P9-BIY-574

To My Good Friend
Mrs. Bobby L. Barnes
A man that I'm Honor to know
and call my friend.
I wish you G-D Blessing In your
Life, and Good luck and Success
In your Life's undertaking.
G-D Bless you and yours

Dr. Degmun A. Faulkenthin

Faulkenstein's Theories
Are Loose on Earth

Faulkenstein's Theories Are Loose on Earth

by

Dezmon A. Faulkenstein, Msc.D.

VANTAGE PRESS
New York / Washington / Atlanta
Los Angeles / Chicago

FIRST EDITION

All rights reserved, including the right of
reproduction in whole or in part in any form.

Copyright © 1982 by Dezmon A. Faulkenstein

Published by Vantage Press, Inc.
516 West 34th Street, New York, New York 10001

Manufactured in the United States of America
ISBN: 533-04690-4

Library of Congress Catalog Card No.: 80-51431

I dedicate my theories to God, who I believe created man and bestowed within him the skill of imagination, from which, if cracked open, some wisdom will spring. And to God who touched and awakened the deep unknown forces of penmanship within me and who stirred me and kissed my imagination to write such a work.

To my children, Rhonda Lee, Dezmon Judah, Zenobia Elaine, and Cawayne Jubar, may you not only grow up to be adults, but stand up as adults.

To Officer Frank Serpico, who is still in exile, Boagarde Lockhart, who was imprisoned and later committed to an asylum, and to Buford Pusser and his wife, who were killed.

To the citizens of the state of Delaware and the people of the United States of America, may you also remember my exile.

To all my enemies, this book is just the beginning, and in time may you come to respect me.

And to all of those who champion the rights of others.

Contents

Acknowledgments

Special thanks to my father, my teacher, the honorable Bernard W. Johns, without whom this book would not have been published.

To my mother, of blessed memory, Miss Anna Mae Johns, who laughed when saying that her son was either a madman or a genius.

To the special ladies Mary Cephes and Georgia Fawcett, who gave me their trust, counsel, and friendship and who ached with me through these past seven years.

To Miss Gerlena Cephes, who took me in out of the cold and the snow.

To the ladies who typed for me and took a chance on me: Helen Baynard and Patricia Sparks, but most of all, Patricia Kemske.

To all my family members may this book be a better understanding of me, and I hope that we may once again become a family.

To my brother Sigmond, his wife Edith, and daughter Tracy, I know that you will be proud.

To Mrs. Jasmin C. Greene for her clerical skills and friendship and to the publishers who dared.

And last but not least, to all of those who betrayed and deserted me. But I especially thank all of you, though few, who stuck by me and believed in me.

To Brenda, who divorced me; Lollita, who loved me; Joyce, who denied me; Ellen, who didn't believe in me; Patricia Sparks, who was ashamed of me; Bettina C. Ferguson, who betrayed me; and to the special woman who one day may accept me.

To the family court counselor, Elizabeth Johnson, who gave to me many kind words when I needed them. And Mr. Nuttle, who tried to be fair and understood.

To Dr. Panariello, who treated me this past year and never sent me a bill. And to the following doctors; Leo Sherman, Joe Manello, David Platt, Scarlet, and Lee.

The professional barber, Mr. Dan, of the Walnut St. barber shop, who cut my hair without charge and listened to my gripes.

To John Brooks, Lillian Richardson, Velma Starling, and Albert Einstein of blessed memory.

To my uncle, William Fleming, of high learning, who taught me the love of reading, learning, independent thinking, and open-mindedness.

To my teacher and friend, Herman Walker, for his instructions in the fields of physics, astronomy, philosophy, science, and mathematics, I am proud and honored to add his name.

To Mr. Wayne Trader, who is a genius yet to be discovered.

To the rabbis, Jacob Kraft, David Geffen, Maxwell Farber, and Able Respis.

And to all Jew and Gentile scholars, intellectuals, and scientists who are dedicated to the promotion of knowledge and learning for all mankind.

To Judge Sidney J. Clark, who proved himself to be a friend.

A Special Appeal

The author wishes to extend his deepest apologies to all Christians and non-Christians who may feel offended by the theories and to other religionists throughout the world who are worshipping the 3,601 invented and created gods known to man, for man, by man.

Which has led me to believe that man out of his own mind and imagination has created God and gods in his own image.

And ye shall be as God knowing good and Evil (Gen. 3:5).

What Is a Genius?

The genius is that one person from out of the un-ordinary, with ideas and things. The average person would say, "Oh, he's so smart," but the genius knows this isn't the case at all; it's just that the average person is so stupid. Then the averagers will call the genius's ideas and things madness, but the genius will call the averagers human because they are only being themselves. In so being, they do not understand.

Dezmon A. Faulkenstein, Msc. D.
December 1, 1972

Notes

Please note the title M = T = CG ÷ sec.; throughout the theory I mention "M" for Mass. I'm speaking strictly of the body of the things and not in a nuclear or atomic sense. Also, "M" would and is mostly referring to matter itself and all and every material known and unknown to us. *Mass in the theory is speaking of the body of things known to us, and therefore our universe, being inside the celestial globe with the masses of things keeping their form until changed by time or something, would and does stay together in its individual makeup. Because time with its velocity of two to three times that of light, 372,000 to 558,000 miles per second,* holds them together, and not as we believe, that the atoms of these matters, with some electromagnetic force, packed tightly, keeps them together in some sense or another. However, I believe as science states, that *all matter is composed of less than 100 or 104 elements and that elements are the fundamental building blocks making up all matter.* Elements are substances that cannot be broken down into anything simpler by ordinary chemical means. However, time or T = M = M.E.C. = G has made a molecular model of all matter, mass, and energy known and unknown to us from the smallest cathoderay up to what I call the Meta-pseudo-micro-macrocosmos, meaning beyond the deceptive small microcosmos and solar system to the larger one, macro, as stated in the theory. *The model molecule of our whole makeup of things could go in this fashion*: (1) All matter consisting of elements basic 104 or etc.; (2) particles of elements consisting of atoms; atoms are the building unit of matter; (3) individual atoms of an element may have different masses; (4) basic of matter; solids, liquids, gas, and I venture to say, powder and flesh. *Chemists have found that all complex substances are mixtures of chemical compounds. Nearly a million compounds have been identified and these, in turn, are merely different combinations of all chemical elements known to science.* As we know we can neither manufacture nor destroy matter; all we can do is to change it from one form to another by chemical process *or time itself;* (5) energy: besides matter, there are other things we deal with in physics, a form or forms different from matter. *Where matter takes up space, energy does not; energy such as electricity, light, sound, and heat.* However, energy on this plane can be divided into many sources of use, as we know. Also, energy combined, such as light, sound, heat, and electricity, plus the energy of all chemical elements, along with the atomic numbers of atoms known to us and more probably unknown to us. The massive energic cell, M. E. C. = G or God out of the ages unknown and unaccountable by us with our primitive number system. *Time and God came together into existence at the same time—* note $T = M. E. C. = G$—forming our universe as we know it and the meta-pseudo-micro-macrocosmos still to be explored by us or others and forming, as well, all life as we know it. So the letter "M," in the theory of $M = T = CG \div$ sec., refers more to matter than atomic mass, or we could say that *mass content of matter depends on the amount of elements within it.* So this would letter or entitle $M = T = CG \div$ sec. into $M + M$, mass plus matter, or matter plus mass, because they are in a sense one and the same, depending as I said, on the chemical element therein. *Therefore, I didn't feel that the time $M + M = T = CG \div$ sec. was necessary.*

I've also wondered what would *be in between a basic atomic structural makeup of an electron, proton, neutron, and pure energy of light, electricity, heat, and high generation of sound?* Could there be a higher form of some magnetic field unknown to us?

As we have in chemistry the molecular structure of the elements, so is our universe made up on a similar plane, such as the molecular structure of our suns, satellites, or planets, cosmic chemical dust, and quasars. *They are all linked to a gigantic molecular structure in the whole and entire universe.* As all molecules have their activity and various movements and forms, so does the molecular structure of elements of the cosmic and astronomical plane. Linking thus one *to another, possibly fulfilling Nobel Prize winners, physicists, Tsung Dao Lee and Dhen Ning Yang, Law of Conservation of Parity (p), which had assumed the symmetry of the universe and suggested instead that space has a kind of twist.*

Also, note this important correction in the theory of M = T = CG ÷ sec. I've stated that time is the celestial globe in the diameter of a circle of 200 decillion miles. The 200 decillion miles applies only to the CG ÷ sec., celestial globe with the velocity of two to three times that of light. This celestial globe is the meta-pseudo-micro-macrocosmos compared to Einstein's microcosmos of 200 sextillion miles. *But when I speak of time itself, I would say that it would be circular or elliptical, with a diameter of 200 decillion light years with a velocity of two to three times that of light, 372,000 to 558,000 miles per second.* This form of time is also applied to M. E. C. = G and T = M. E. C. = G. *Yes, I would venture to say that God and time are one and the same,* or M. E. C. = G and T = M. E. C. = G. Also, God and time in physics is abstractional, so, therefore, in science and as a scientist, I would say that God is M. E. C. = G, a massive energic cell equals God. *This massive energic cell is as big as time, 200 decillion light years.*

Note: Whenever the author's theories appear in the text, they should be interpreted as follows:

M = T = CG ÷ sec. (mass equals time equals a celestial globe divided by seconds)

T = M. E. C. = G (time equals a massive energic cell equals God)

M. E. C. = God (massive energic cell equals God)

T + A. E. A. = N (time plus an abstract energic atom equals nature)

Introduction: Legopsytric Neurosis

From the Latin, meaning the, or a, strong belief in hallucinations or illusions.

I must admit that anything and everything man makes, makes up, or lays his hand to or mind to, is not perfect. Nor is it absolute. One way or another, there is an imperfection in it somewhere, though hard to find, that imperfection will come to light sooner or later. This is what has happened in the many fields of study that we take so much for granted these days. History has shown us this: (1) man may have believed in One God. *Now, as Michael Eyguem DeMontaigne, the fifteenth century scholar has shown us, man now believes in 3,601 gods.* So, first, we had the Bible account, written, handed down, and taught by man that God created man in His own image. *But now the history of man, according to the account of DeMontaigne, man has created and worshipped the gods in his own image.* (2) Then, historically, man once believed that the earth was square, according to bibliology. And the angels, he said, stood on the four corners of the earth, (Rev. 7:1), *implying that the earth was square.* (3) There was the time when man thought that the earth was a straight line and if a person took to sea in a ship, he would row off the end of the earth. (4) In early medieval history, up until the middle of the twentieth century, alchemists were warlocks and witches and thus burned at the stake or beheaded. But we know and see them, today as early scientists. (5) There were cases of insane people, who were possessed of the devil and thus put away or put to death. (6) And there was the case of early people suffering from disease and being cured. (7) *Jesus Christ,* being in the form of man, was God and at the same time the Son of God but under the powers of three God heads, the Father, the Son, and the Holy Ghost.

Now what I have done is given you some of the few examples, out of the many cases of the history of man, or what he strongly believed in. But now I will attempt to give you seven more case histories of our era that we, with our primitive minds and intellect, still cling and adhere to, though the other seven have been disproved and we no longer adhere to them. *Here are seven of the many great stories, fairy tales, lies, and myths that so-called modern man accepts and believes*:

1.   Jesus Christ was God, incarnate, and that God has three god heads, Father, Son, and Holy Ghost. He came to remove all sin from the world, would establish peace, and died for the same. Whosoever will believe in Him will be saved, and for those who don't, they will be damned. In short, whoever didn't would go to hell. Now this story and lie is just one of the many. This God or Sun God is just another of the *3,600 made, invented, believed in, and worshipped by man and modern man*. Though Jesus was supposed to have risen, still *man has not basically changed, if anything, He is worse*. Even though Jesus may have died for the sins of man, still man is sinning, *and there has been no peace*. If anything, there have been forty-four major wars. Though Jesus was supposed to have died, He wouldn't remain dead for the account of the story or myth. He took his life back again; *this is the same as A slaps B and knocks B's tooth out*. Then A tells B how sorry he is and pays him 10 dollars for the tooth, but then A comes back three days later and takes back the 10 dollars.

2.   Sin—our account of the fall of man and the coming of sin by a snake and a woman, though the Bible does not really say that the fruit was an apple, just the tree of knowledge of good and evil. Then we have the Greek account of Pandora's box, which contained all the evils of the world but was opened and let out, thus, we have all the sins and evils to this day. And Pandora's box contained all the good.

3.   Politics war, religion, and law are necessary and are for

keeping man in check. But look at the matter closely. Politics has never been the answer but one of the greatest lies, and to prove this, look at it from its earliest beginnings up until today and you can answer this questions for yourself.

War! War will be until man, science, and philosophy, metaphysics and "metaphysicotheologocosmologingology," as well as mathematics, are in harmony. Well, in long years to come, though long we'll be above such folly, childishness, and primitiveness. If all politicians make peace and not war, they would soon be out of a job.

Religion! Religion, as Ralph Waldo Emerson once said, *is a disease of the mind, and thus, it, too, has inflicted many lies on man, mankind, and society.* This was once remarked upon by Bertrand Russell, in his book *Why I Am Not A Christian.*

Law! Law is worse than them all because it is a mixture of the three just mentioned and has nothing organized of itself. *If it were not for sin, politics, war, and religion, law would not exist.*

Our educational system! *It is as primitive now as it will be in the future if not changed.* The institutions of learning are in part teaching us how to make a living *but for the most part not teaching us how to live.* Also, any person who goes there will find that he or she is being trained for some specific field, but outside of that field they are intellectually short and can think or speak of very little. If they should indulge in some form of conversation, they are lost and don't really know what they are talking about, while in their own field of work and study, they find that to others they are really a bore. So what we need in our schools today is not education but reeducation.

Materialism! We find many people all over the world believing that the more materialistic a person is the more successful that person is, and the same for themselves, if applied the same. When you really look at it, modern man will work like a dog and go through many changes to gather and store up his supplies. He is never, and can never be satisfied unless he changes from materialism and works for his basic needs. Materialism, more than anything we know, is the main motivating factor in the life and work of man.

God! God is the oldest thing in the history of man *and still man does not really and factually know Who created whom.* But they continue to go on to believe the religions or not believe —the atheist—or just simply wonder (the agnostic).

Time, space, universe, energy, mass, matter, etc., are still keeping man busy as always, but still he has made little progress even though he may pride himself in thinking that he has made great headway. And because of this, I, Dezmon Faulkenstein, have been forced to see many things that man has long been neglecting to see. Such as: (1) *there is no modern man* due to the fact that I believe and I am not alone in my belief that man is the most primitive form of life in the universe, though he may pride himself in thinking that he is the highest form on earth. (2) Man is still, with his so-called skills and technology, backward and primitive. *He can send objects into outer place, or what we call outer space, but at the same time cannot get along on the earth and on earth study; he knows less about himself than about machines.* (3) If one man kills another, he says that it is wrong, but then society will publicly hang, shoot, or kill the murderer in some way, though killing him will not bring his victim back. But we as men say, think, teach, and believe that we are modern and have a so-called higher form of living, which we call civilization. *We are in what we call the twenty-first century and still have Indians on a reservation. Are we modern and civilized?* We still have capital punishment of some form or other and with all this so-called religion, politics, and education, we still can't get along with one another but fight and kill, segregate and discriminate and hate one another.

Are we civilized and modern? Man still needs his old gods of 3,601 or more, plus old fairy tales, myths, and backward ideas, yet we are civilized and modern? (4) Man, according to the Psychological Foundation and other organizations, man is *suffering from 250 or more phobias,* meaning: that our modern civilized man, as you call him, is suffering from 250 or more fears. And modern man today, if you look at him, is suffering from four major ones: (1) black-ta-phobia—that is, people who are afraid of blacks. (2) White-ta-phobia, those who, in return, fear whites. (3) Religia-phobia, those who fear another's religion, and the preaching and teaching of the end of the world, hell and damnation, and (4) nuclear-phobia, ninety-nine percent fear of man's worries and praying conceded a clash or nuclear warfare between the nations, thus blowing us all to hell or sending us God knows where. Yes, modern and civilized man, as you call yourselves and would have others, and mislead others, to believe that we are up to date. But let me tell you that we are just as backward and primitive as we were thousands of years ago. *The only difference is that we have the age of the machine, but still our machines are primitive, too, as the four theories will show you.* If you want to know just how primitive and backward we are, then I challenge you and your whole species to understand, believe, protect, and accept.

1. $M + T = CG \div$ sec. Mass $=$ time $=$ celestial globe divide by seconds
2. $M.\ E.\ C. = G$ The massive Energic cell $=$ God
3. $T = M.\ E.\ C. = G$ Time $=$ The massive energic cell $=$ God
4. $T + A.N.A. = N$ Time plus an abstract energic atom equals nature.

1. These theories could lead to some of the understanding of body, mass, matter, and energy, deportation, and transplantation, meaning, you will in time be able to disassemble your body's mass of atoms from one point and then reassemble them again, meaning to disappear or reappear from different points at will. And the same holds true for objects.

2. And let's say if you wanted to get a book from the table, you would only have to concentrate a little and thus force it to come to you; you would have very little need for telephones because you would only have to concentrate a little; the one whom you are trying to contact will carry on a telepathic conversation hundreds of miles away.

3. If you should cut yourself or inflict a wound anywhere on your body, then you would have only to use once again your powers given to you, which you now use very little, and the wound would quickly heal.

4. Doors would open and close at your will; your cars, planes, and trains would be of no use to you because of your energic body atoms' transportation, and much much more. You, when tired, will not have to lie down and sleep but just stand still and concentrate and, at the snap of a finger, refresh yourself. You will need no courts of law, and no policeman, lawyers, jails, etc. *Man will be above these trivial and primitive things. You will need no hospitals or doctors, as you know them; no undertakers, because you will be able, in all these cases, to use your brain to the highest form and know how to manipulate your atoms, when need be.* You will have no need to lock your door because you will have no need for it. You will have one religion, and that will be what you are reading, plus the four formula theorems. By then, you should have fulfilled the Bible statement, that God gave man dominion over the earth, though now you have this dominion but one man competing against the other, which is foolish and primitive. In time, we will learn how to use the four formula theorems, and this will be your modern civilized state of higher life and harmony in and with the universe. Now we are the lowest form of life in the universe; on earth, we are the highest form, but still backward, uncivilized, nonmodern and primitive.

Fantastic and impossible you say? Yes, you would because you are still primitive and backward. When you start to do some of these things and use the theories, you will then and only then come into the modern and civilized age.

Faulkenstein's Theories
Are Loose on Earth

1

The Old and New Concept of Time

Man, first of all, governs his time existence according to years upon years, and this is a big era. The life span of man is so short and quick that even he has failed to see just how short. First of all, time is a thing that measures all things, yet all things can't measure it. Since time is as big to man as God in conception and perception, man has formed his own account of it into many numbers and formulas, such as hours, days, weeks, months, years, centuries, decades, and eons. But this is not so. Time may be given all these names, but still man does not really live in these eras, though he accounts them as such. *It is my belief that man's life is about, or shorter than, the time of an average blinking of your eye. Man lives seconds within that single split second and no more.* The reason for my theory is that its not because time goes on but also that it is moving so very, very fast that we, with our small mind, can't catch it. Therefore, we try in some way to catch up with it or account by numerical form or extend its existence by numerical account, such as backward, forward, or present. The backward account, we call past; the forward account, we call future; the present, we call now. We haven't noticed it before, but everything that happens in time *happens within seconds*, though we label these important seconds as days, weeks, months, years, etc. One lives within these seconds, though we say he was two, three, or thirty years old. We eat, sleep, walk, laugh, cry, love, kill, and help one another in a split second. What we fail to see is that these split seconds make up seconds, seconds into minutes, they into hours, days, weeks, months, years, and on and on. *It all boils down to seconds and split seconds.* Time, we think, is so big to us, therefore, we say we don't really know it.

Allow me to give you a form of understanding. Just stand still right now and blink your eye, an average blink. Now as you blink, think of how quick this is, *you only live possibly that one blink.* Now take a piece of paper and write 60 seconds to a minute, 60 minutes = one hour; 24 hours = one day; 7 days = one week; 4 weeks = one month; 12 months = one year and stop; 360 days. *Yet we are living within seconds, within a single second and can't reach one minute.* How much more *an hour, day, week, month or year?* These are only words and numbers used to stretch time. It is moving so fast, and we are thinking so *slowly and small.* Now write out the seconds theory: 60 seconds to a minute; 60 minutes to a hour; 24 hours to a day; 7 days to a week; 4 weeks to a month; and 12 months to a year.

Sixty seconds is an exceptional life span of anything; one hour = *3,600,000* seconds; 24 hours = *86,400,000* seconds; one week = *602,800,000;* one month = *2,411,200,000;* and one year = *28,934,400,000* seconds. This is what makes time so infinite because it is like this: man must use his devices for words and numbers to explain time, count it, and stretch it. Now don't say this is impossible because we have been using the hour, day, week, month, and year for so long that we may find it hard to conceive the seconds theory. For example: here is an electric globe. It shines with a white light. But suppose I paint the globe an opaque black? If it is night and I have no other light in the room, darkness results. But the light does not cease. Within the light globe, the light shines just as it did before. But the light can no longer express itself as light to your eyes. To an ignorant mind, it seems that no light is present, but the light is still there.

Now I scratch a small circle of the black paint from the light globe. Just that much light then shines through. As I keep on scraping paint from the globe, the volume of light grows. The light represents your mental concept of the time theory.

Your life is the channel for the expression of power through oneness with the universal mind. *Modern science tells us that there are no lights in the rays thrown out by the sun until those rays reach the atmosphere of our earth.* Likewise, there is no light in electricity until the energy reaches a globe or some material object that can manifest its incandescence. No light shines from universal mind power until human lives and human thoughts are attuned to that expression.

No man yet knows what electricity is; that the average man in many ways does not know what electricity is or fully understand it doesn't mean it does not exist or there is no such thing. Again, vibration. Let us content ourselves by saying that light and electricity, as the servants of men, are an unknown energy carrying limitless POWER, drawn from the atmosphere, pulsating at a tremendous vibration rate.

If you think back on some religion and scientific writings, would we be right in quoting the Bible as saying, "that one day is with the lord as a thousand years and a thousand years as one day" (2 Pet. 3:8). Also, Ps. 90:4; "For a thousand years in thy sight are but as yesterday when it is past, and as a watch in the night." *MD magazine* (published by M.D. Publications, vol. 12, no. 11, p. 9, 1968) states, in an article by Félix Martí Ibáñez, that:

"Has the universe changed? No, the universe has not changed throughout the course of history; what has changed is only mental attitude toward the universe. Life has existed for three billion years; man has existed for about a million years; he has made use of his brain for his own progress for about fifty thousand years and has been able to record his thoughts for about six thousand years; but man has been using science as an education a factor for only about 300 years."

So if we use the seconds theory, what must change is our mental attitude totward our universe, time conception, and perception, however hard that it may be. *How fast is fast?* "Fast" is a word that is growing more relative as science grows more complex. Working with laser pulses, scientists have discovered time

3

intervals that are difficult to relate to our normal experience: *Nanoseconds, picoseconds, and femtoseconds*—that's fast talking.

The blink of an eye is the shortest interval in ordinary experience. It normally lasts about *two-tenths of a second. A jet traveling at 600 miles per hour goes about 175 feet during a blink.* But in an interval of 40 nanoseconds—one billionth of a second— that same plane travels a distance equal to about the thickness of this paper.

Scientists can break down *the nanosecond* into shorter intervals called *picoseconds.* Here the jet plane fails as an example, and we must refer to the speed of light—186,000 miles per second in a vacuum—the highest possible speed according to the theory of relativity. *In one picosecond, light travels a little over one-hundredth of an inch.*

One one-thousandth of a picosecond is a femtosecond, but we don't have to worry about that. With further probing into subatomic events, even this tiny piece of time may one day become as useful as the ticking of a clock.

Anyone who has experienced an accident frequently describes the incident as having occurred within a "split second." It certainly is true that accidents happen quickly, and some occur probably within the time intervals described to remove ourselves from exposure; thus injuries occur. Another way to look at the seconds theory is that time to man is like a big spinning top with man inside the top while spinning; he, therefore, cannot picture the top in motion because he is turning with the motion. Now if he could step out of the top and look at it from the outside instead of being on the inside trying to account for the movement, he would have and see a different picture of time and therefore see how fast time is and how slow his conception of this inside it. It is not just the world, planet, and the other planets along with the moon, sun, and stars that are spinning and moving very, very fast but the whole thing, *the whole cosmos.* All of this, too, is inside the top and therefore hinders us from the conception of it. Even when we fly in a plane and look down, we notice how much smaller and smaller things on the earth get as we go higher. We are still inside time, and we are still inside

4

the top. When we watch a rocket go up and up until we can't see with the unaided eye, the rocket is still inside the top and those inside the rocket or space ship watching it go into outer space, how much smaller and smaller the earth gets. They are still in the top. *The only thing that has changed is their mental outlook on these matters, though the matters themselves remain the same.* What changes this is that we, by natural motion, are spinning with the top. With locomotion of any sort, train, bus, car, plane, rocket, spinning at a higher speed and going so much faster but not as fast as the top. We are going fast but not really; in the amazement of it all, we only imagine so. The example of this is a man standing still and a race car going about 100 miles per hour passing him; he thinks it is going fast, but the same man watching two cars at the same speed but passing one another at different directions in a criss-cross motion, would think that they are going even faster. This is due to the fact that they are in their own kind of top and he is on the outside looking in, while they in the car or top have a different opinion. The same holds true of sound.

All space is vibrating with sound, from the farthest star that swings blind and blackening in the darkness of the interstellar space waves of vibrations, too tremendously above our poor human limits of forty thousand vibrations per second for us to hear them.

Our human senses are rigidly confined within narrow limitations. We are both deaf and blind to these vaster rates of vibration. *When these vibrations reach the astounding rate of four hundred thousand millions, we see them in the form of light.*

There is boundless creative opportunity and untold power in God's great universe for the use of that hitherto unknown vibration of your invisible self—the mind, which we call thought.

Human mind creates human destiny. "And ye shall know the truth and the truth shall make you free," said the Galilean in the Bible. One great and simple truth will make you not only free but will also make you the master of your own destiny. That one truth is that your own mind created every circumstance of your human existence except, perhaps, birth and death.

The same mind of yours controls the results of every condition in your life.

We live in a big top that has other tops within it and therefore cannot perceive clearly the seconds element. (Using the seconds element with time, it is on the same basis as the speed of light.) *The speed of time is at least two to three times faster than the speed of light,* the speed of light being 186,000 miles per second, while *the speed of time is 372,000 to 558,000 miles per second.* You know why? *Light, too, is traveling in that same top called time and not out of it; also, anything outside of the top doesn't exist.* All and every kind of existence is inside the spinning top called time.

The sun, as modern science has shown us, is the center of the universe, but before this the earth was the center of the universe. It was supposed to be surrounded by nine spheres of invisible space, the first seven carrying the "planets" as then known: (1) Diana, or the moon, (2) Mercury, (3) Venus, (4) Apollo, or the sun, (5) Mars, (6) Jupiter, and (7) Saturn. The eighth, the starry sphere, carried the fixed stars, and the ninth, the crystalline sphere, was added by Hipparchus in the second century B.C. to account for the precession of the equinoxes. Finally, in the Middle Ages, was added a solid barrier that enclosed the universe and shut it off from nothingness and the empyrean. These last two spheres carried neither star nor planet.

This brings us to a closed opinion, to the statement that life is short, but according to the split second theory, life is shorter than that.

Time is also round, a complete circle and not straight out into infinity. For time, like what it is traveling in, is a complete circle forming the spinning top and not a straight line. The time spinning top goes round and around, on, on, and on; this is infinity.

Now there are some who would think or even agree that my theory is the same, or in some respects similar to, that of Einstein's theory of $E = mc^2$. I admit that in some ways it is, but with the exception of *two things:* (1) My theory is centered around the way man calculates time and his place in it and the

6

speed of things in relation to time and light. (2) *The difference between the speed and movement of time and light.* Now Einstein and others would state that *light moves with time,* wherefore, *I believe that light does not—only within it.* For something to move within something doesn't necessarily mean it is moving exactly with it per se or at the same time with it; *one could be moving faster than the other.* This could be explained in this wise: a horse, a wagon; the wagon is attached to the horse, and the horse is running very fast, the wagon right along with him. Though they both are going at the same time, *they are both not going at the same speed* even though it would appear so. If they had a point to reach, the horse would reach there first, the wagon immediately following. If the horse moved backward at any given speed the wagon would be going faster and would reach the point first, depending on the location of the point, even though motivated by the horse. A man driving a car; though the car is motivated by the man, the man being in the car, the point or front of the car would reach a point before the man driving it, with the back of it following. The reason for this is that *we have in these cases two to three different intervals, though one is attached to the other.*

It is the same thing with the speed of time, having the speed of light attached to it but inside it. Therefore, the speed of light, we are taught and told, travels 186,000 per second, but with the seconds theory, the speed of time, being two to three times faster than that of light, would be 372,000 to 558,000 per second, or split second. To give an example of the speed of time being faster than the speed of light and light traveling within or inside time and not as fast: The case of a man spinning a wheel. But now the man is turning the wheel, and his hand moves around and around, but note the wheel, too, is going around and around but only faster than the hand turning it. This relation is the same as that of the front wheels of a car to those of the back, though they are attached to the same object. It is the same with the spinning top of time, along with the speed of light traveling inside it, and everything else within.

Now the theory goes on to explain itself about mass and

time. But one may question *What about the celestial globe?* Well, I used this globe because it is the finest example of the mass and time barrier that we are in. The celestial globe, as we know, is a ball within the earth, as a small ball that sometimes could act as the sun inside the center of the larger globe. This type of globe consists of seven to nine rings which act as spheres of the universe. These spheres are distances of space from the center of a point having the same measurement from all points back to the center. Another way of understanding the big spinning top is to look at it in the form of a big kaleidoscope with everything turning or spinning inside it, with all the planets, suns, and the billion, million, and thousands of miles between them, and all things known and unknown to us, seen and unseen to us, beginning and completing their own individual cycle at one time or at the same time.

But then, too, one could ask the question *If Faulkenstein's Theory states we have no such thing as a minute, known to us only our practice of stretching of time by numerical form,* or words to the same meaning, *how then is it that we have night and day or our four seasons, as it may be?* Well, in answer to this, I would say that our night and days and our four seasons could be explained in this wise. To us, night and day, as we know them, consist of twenty-four hours, and these days are stretched into months that will eventually stretch into years, as we know them. *But with the time theory*, this is all a matter of split seconds, within split seconds, happening so fast that our small minds cannot grasp the quickness of the event. If we could, then, our days and nights, our four seasons, would be as if someone were flickering an electric switch on and off as fast as they could, bringing us flash after flash. (If you would right now take a light switch and flick it on and off, then you could see the quickness of the light within a matter of seconds, then you will have a better understanding of how our night and day and seasons are doing the same thing but going even faster.) Our day and night would be in the time theory or split-second theory, as it is also called, a matter of split seconds and not twenty-four hours. *Our four seasons are all a matter of seconds,* and not, on the average, ninety days each, as we know them. The reason for all of this is that we, our night and day and seasons, are each inside the top of *time, moving at the rate of 372,000 to 558,000 miles per second,* two to three times the velocity of light. Therefore, we do not have night and day *but light and darkness* and seasons, not three months each, but they run all within seconds only.

My theory also leads me to believe spiritually that God did not create the universe, heavens and the earth, plus the elements of day and night in a twenty-four hour day, *but in possibly 6,000 years. A thousand years for each creation.* In 2 Pet. 3:8 and Ps. 90:14, "One day is with the Lord as a thousand years and a thousand years as one day." So God is almighty and is bigger in *idea* than we can see, conceive, or understand. So, spiritually and metaphysically, there is a different time element with God than there is with man, *possibly an unknown time element not known to us.* So If one would apply the seconds theory to that of the Bible statement of a thousand years as one day with God, and if by chance God did do this in 6,000 years, making nothing too impossible for him, then the seconds theory would have him to have formed *the six creations within a 86,400,000 seconds period, equaling a twenty-four hour day as we know it. The total of the six creations would be 518,400,000 seconds,* but still many would find this to be far factual. For they may find the second theory as hard to believe as that of the Bible statement of a thousand years to God as one day. The Bible refers to God and not man. *My seconds theory* points out the element of *time itself,* not man. For in both theories, man is of God, and man is of time. So both of these I believe to be too big for man to understand. The first principle that brings all things into being (that philosophers call God) is that infinite period of space, called time, a mystery to man. Therefore, he finds it hard at times, no matter what his intellect may be, to believe in them both, though, while living he is, in one way or another, coexisting with them both. Job 26:1-14 and Isa. 40:18-22, written in the eighth century before the common era, or B.C., states that the world is a circle or the earth, and my theory supports this but states that time itself has a form and is in a form of a circle, *a big unimaginative spinning top going at 372,000 to 558,000 miles per second.*

And, too, the split-second theory shows that we outlive one blink of an eye; it also shows in the long run that we live much longer and, at the same time, we are much older. For example, *if we use the time system that we now have in relation to us, the time theory shows that one second to us equals two to three years,* depending on the velocity of the top we're now in. At two times the velocity of light, *the time top's velocity is 372,000 miles per second; so one second to us would be two years; 60 seconds = 120 years; 1 hour = 7,200 years; 1 day = 172,800 years. So in this wise, do I mean that he would never live and does not live a day as we know it?* If the velocity of the time top would be *three times* that of light, equaling *558,000 miles per second, then one second would be 3 years; 60 seconds = 180 years; 1 hour = 10,800 years, and 1 day = 259,200 years. So you see, if we accept time as we know it, we would not hardly live an hour* at the velocity of light and time at 372,000 to 558,000 miles per second.

But then, too, it also shows us how we really have misused and misunderstood time. At the same time, the split-second theory shows us just what kind of time barrier we are really in, without knowing it before. In reality, we are much older and at the same time live longer than we think. *To find out how old you are,* apply the time theory to your age as you know it. By doing the following at the velocity of twice the speed of light (372,000 miles per second.) 1 second = 2 years; 60 seconds = 120 years; 1 hour = 7,200 years; *and 1 day = 172,800 years.* Then "X" plus your age as you know it, such as, eighteen years old. In the time or split-second theory you may be 3,112,400 years old. If the velocity of the time top is three times the velocity of light (558,000 miles per second), then 1 second = 3 years; 60 seconds = 180 years; 1 hour = 10,800 years, and 1 day = 259,200 years. Then "X" plus your age, 18, or whatever it may be, can be counted as demonstrated above, and then you will come up with your actual age.

In reference to this, would we still find this hard to believe?

What about the man-made objects that can travel two to three times the speed of sound? Science states that the speed of sound is 750 miles per hour. Guided missiles travel three times this velocity (2,250 miles per hour). Why should we find it hard to believe in the velocity of the speed of time being two to three times faster than the speed of light. The argument over whether the velocity of light was infinite or finite brought about some hard and heated arguments during the Middle Ages between two most renowned scientists or scholars of that era, none other than Descartes and Galileo. Descartes (1596-1650), claiming it to be infinite, while Galileo (1564-1642), claimed it to be finite. But my concern here is not as to which of these great men was right or wrong but in what relation has the velocity of light to that of the celestial globe of time or the kaleidoscope spinning form of time, compared to the velocity of light. For I believe that light inside this big spinning celestial globe and the kaleidoscope-of-time are both of the same, finite and infinite. My reason for this is that it is first finite due to the fact that time is the main factor and light the second. Time has within itself all things known or unknown to us, in which light is only one of them, though, at the same time, light is very important to us. So light, being not itself but a part of time and measured out by it, makes it finite. On the other hand, light, being what we accept as the fastest thing known to us, outside of my seconds theory, we naturally say that it is infinite. But when we consider the second and split-second theory, we can see the big spinning top, globe or kaleidoscope, with light traveling inside of it, with the top, globe, or the kaleidoscope turning on, on, on, and light being unable to travel outside of it and at the same time along with it, makes light infinite.

2

Space and Light
Space According to Some Great Men and Their Ideas

Now I would also venture to say that the earth, sun, moon and the planets, known and unknown to us, have their own individual pattern of movement along with their own sun and moons within the big Spinning top of time and do not venture out of it or from it but continue on its own course, unchangeable. The only thing that would cause them not to do so is if the spinning top therein would slow down and if the TOP would come to a complete stop or if they themselves would over a period of time die out.

Scientists believe that *light will go* completely around the earth *in a seventh of a second*, and *it takes about eight minutes for the sunlight to travel the 93,000,000 from the sun to the earth.* Then in the morning, when the sun comes up, it has actually risen eight minutes before. In this respect, no one on the earth sees the sun come up. So since it takes eight minutes for the sunlight to travel from the sun to the earth, we can say that the sun is eight minutes away by light in the same way as we could say that Stamford is forty miles from New York City by rail. The nearest star to us beyond the sun is *Alpha-Centauri*, which is about *four light years away*. This means that it would take us four light years to get there if we traveled by light. Now science tells us that *one light year is 6,000,000,000,000 miles*. So Alpha-Centauri is about *24,000,000,000,000 miles away*, which is a long way for a next-door neighbor.

Einstein's theory of relativity, applied to that of relative motion, states that the behavior of light waves was not influenced in any way by the movement of the earth through space. So the the same should apply to the big spinning top of time, with the speed of light traveling through it. *For the speed of time is not in any way influenced by the speed of light per se. Time is two to three times faster than the speed of light* (372,000 to 558,000 miles per second).

Now allow me to give you a little understanding of Einstein's special theory of relativity. This theory of Einstein's shows that in the relativity of objects, compared or relative to the speed of light, the object moves at a constant velocity, relative to an observer and the behavior of light waves. This can best be done by having the observer describe the object while it is moving at a constant velocity relative to him. The peculiar behavior of light waves will markedly influence the description since it is the reflection of the light waves from the object to the observer that enables him to see and to describe the object.

Assuming we have two identical rockets, A and B, traveling with a finite velocity relative to each other out in space, A and B are each equipped with at least the most elementary scientific instruments, particularly measuring sticks and clocks, and it is especially important that these be compared beforehand so that A's be identical with B's. When the analysis begins, B is passing A, both their clocks read the same time, and nearby supernova explodes at the same instant. Neither A nor B is aware that the star has exploded since the light waves of the explosion haven't reached them yet.

A short time later, the light waves from the explosion reach A and B, but when they do, A and B will be separated by the distance X. From the second postulate, A and B see the light waves coming in with the same velocity relative to each and, *letting C represent the velocity of light waves for A* and C^1 that for B, we can say that $C = C^1$. The distance of the explosion from each, d and d¹, and the times given by each of their clocks, t and t¹, are then incorporated, and the analysis proceeds to interrelate their distance from each other, their relative velocities, their respective times, the velocity of light, etc.

The resulting equations are called *the Lorentz transformation equations* because Lorentz had previously arrived at the same equations on the basis of his theory. However, his theory was artificial, being based on the necessary existence of the other, and was not logically consistent. *Then, too, some of his results applied only to electric and magnetic fields.* The special theory of relativity, on the other hand, rests solidly on two fundamental postulates, and their results apply to all matter without exception.

Using the Lorentz transformation equations, we can now predict the results each obtains if he scrutinizes the other closely as to length, mass, etc. We now proceed to discuss each of these in detail. And since the postulates involve conclusions contrary to everyday experience and are the basis for this analysis, the reader should not be surprised to find that the results will also be unexpected and seemingly queer. *The reason the theory of relativity is in general looked upon as being incomprehensible is not because the results are difficult to understand but that they are difficult to believe.*

If A is able to measure B's length when they are moving with velocity v relative to each other, the mathematical results predict that B appears to have shrunk. Where L¹ is the length A obtains for B, L is B's original length, v their velocity, and c the velocity of light. As an illustration, if A and B were each of length twenty feet when at rest with respect to each other but *are not separating at a velocity of 93,000 miles per second* (half the velocity of light), then B's apparent length, as measured by A, can be determined by substituting these values in the equation, with the results that A would measure B to be only seventeen feet long. *Or if they were separating at 161,000 miles a second* (about nine-tenths the velocity of light), then, to A, B's length would appear to be only ten feet. Also, since we said that the rockets were identical, their length should be equal if they are not moving with respect to each other at all (relative velocity of zero), and the equation should verify this. It is seen that it does since, when v equals zero, the value of the radical is one and $L^1 = L$. *Hence, with B at rest with respect to A, A would find B to be twenty feet long.*

Now the reader asks, What value does B get if he measures A's length in passing? In this case, the formula still applies, but now L^1 and L should be interchanged since L^1 in reality, is the length seen by the observer doing the measuring. Here, the results are the same, that is, at a separation velocity of 93,000 miles per second, A's rocket will appear to be seventeen feet long. Nor does it matter whether they are separating or approaching—the result is still the same, depending only on their relative velocity.

Now, what if A measures his own length while B is passing? If he does, he would find it to be twenty feet long, since he is not moving with respect to himself. *Of course, it is immaterial whether B is passing at the same time or whether A is moving relative to any other system. A always obtains twenty feet for his length.* Similarly, if B measures his own length while moving or not with respect to A or any other system, he also always obtains twenty feet.

This effect of length contraction can be stated simply: whenever one observer is moving with respect to another, whether approaching or separating, it appears to both observers that everything about the other has shrunk in the direction of motion. Neither observer notices any effect in his own system, however.

It is seen that the contraction effect is appreciable only if the relative velocity is comparable to the velocity of light. Since the velocities with which we are familiar on earth are considerably lower than the velocity of light, we do not ordinarily notice the contraction effect. For example, an airplane moving at a rate of 750 miles an hour relative to an observer would shrink by about a millionth of a millionth of an inch, or about the diameter of the nucleus. Such small amounts are not even detectable with our most precise instruments, let alone being noticed by the human eye.

It may seem to some readers that the preceding discussion is very artificial and, hence, invalid inasmuch as it would be well nigh impossible, actually, to measure the length of a rocket with a ruler as it passes at a velocity of 93,000 miles a second. Then are the conclusions predicted without meaning? The answer is that the conclusion is valid. Although a ruler was used for illustration because it is the simplest devise for measuring length, the results would apply regardless of how the lengths are measured. In an actual experiment, the measuring equipment would be quite complicated, involving electronic circuits, light beams, etc.

For historical reasons, the contraction effect is still referred to as the Fitzgerald-Lorentz contraction and adequately expressed to the now famous limerick:

> There was a young fellow named Fisk
> Whose fencing was exceedingly brisk;
> So fast was his action
> The Fitzgerald contraction
> Reduced his rapier to a disk.

This same theory *I believe can be applied to that of the split-second theory* (compared to our age, how we view the things we see, and so on).

Upon examining the large problems of the detection of the ether and the experiments which had been performed (wherein the properties of light played an important part), Einstein drew two very important conclusions. These are known as the fundamental postulates of the special theory and are the foundation that supports the rest of the theory.

The purpose in this is to discuss both of these postulates in detail and then to present the results that follow if the necessary mathematics were to be carried out using these postulates as the starting point. (The mathematical steps themselves are not included, in keeping with the purpose of the book.)

The first postulate answers the dilemma of the other. Stated simply, it says that the ether cannot be detected. But before we see why not, let us first look at some simple examples that will illustrate Einstein's reasoning in coming to this conclusion. Suppose you find yourself on a bridge over a brook, which is flow-

16

ing slowly by underneath. You are looking down into the water. As you gaze at your reflection in the water, it won't be long before you find it very easy to imagine that it is you and the bridge that are gliding smoothly along and that the water is perfectly calm. Of course, you don't remain in such a trance for long because you just know the bridge is stationary and that it is the water that is moving.

But now we'll consider another example where it will not be so easy to determine which of two objects is moving. Assume you are living in the future when you can hop into your private rocket and take a trip out into space for beyond the earth. You start off straight out from the earth at 5,000 miles an hour with respect to the earth, and you set your controls so you will expect to cruise through space at this speed.

After cruising until the earth is out of sight, you sight another rocket behind you. It swiftly overtakes you. You are surprised that he's going faster than you since you had thought yours was just about the fastest little "hot rock" in the universe. As he passes you, you're even more surprised when he indicates that he thinks you're not even moving! *But how can you prove that you are really moving?* You know that he's moving at a different rate than you are because you see him approaching you. You probably would be equipped with a radar set, similar to those used by the highway police to detect violators of the speed limit, which will tell you that he's moving at 1,000 miles per hour with respect to you. But this is all you can determine.

You might think that since you left the earth, traveling at 5,000 miles an hour, and he's now passing you at 1,000 miles an hour faster, that he is then going 6,000 miles per hour with respect to the earth. But this is not necessarily true. It could also mean that you are now going 2,000 miles per hour with respect to the earth and he is going 3,000 miles an hour with respect to the earth. Or, strange as it may seem, it could even mean that he is not moving backward toward the earth at a rate of 1,000 miles an hour!

You will rapidly conclude that without some "motionless" object to use to measure your velocity, you can never tell which one of you is moving and who is standing, if either. You can only conclude that you are moving at 1,000 miles an hour with respect to your space friend. Nor will it ever be possible for you to develop an instrument, however complicated, that will tell you anything more than that you are moving with respect to something else. Indeed, *if you are ever alone, out in space, far removed from all the stars and planets, with nothing to see as a reference point to measure your speed, you will never know whether you are moving or not!*

It was not this fact that Einstein recognized: all motion is relative (hence, the theory of relativity). We can never speak of absolute motion as such but only of motion relative to something else. *In general, we cannot say that an object has a velocity of such-and-such but must say that it has a velocity of such-and-such relative to so-and-so.* This is not done for objects on the earth because it is understood that their velocities are relative to the earth. A speed limit of fifty miles an hour, for example, is understood to mean fifty miles an hour relative to the earth. *But out away from the earth a velocity by itself has no meaning.*

It is easy to imagine a conversation several hundred years from now between a father and his wandering, space-lustful son. If the father tells him to keep his hot rock under 1,000 miles an hour, the boy might reply in all sincerity, "Relative to what, daddy, the earth or the Big Dipper?"

There is no heavenly body in our universe that we can use as a stationary reference point. The earth rotates on its axis; it travels in its orbit around the sun; the sun and the solar system are moving about within our galaxy, the Milky Way, which is itself rotating. And our galaxy is also moving relative to the other galaxies. The whole universe is filled with movement. And in all this seemingly haphazard turmoil, no one can say what is stationary. We can only say that all heavenly bodies are moving relative to one another, and no one of these is different in this respect.

I would say, according to the seconds theory of time, that on earth and inside the big spinning top, like the man in a spaceship in reference to the special relative theory of Einstein's, that a man, in outer space far removed from all the stars and planets, with nothing to use as a reference point to measure his speed, would never know if he is moving or not due to the fact that when he left earth, he could measure his speed or movement in relation to it. But, in outer space, there is no point or anything relative to him or his space ship by which he can measure. *So this, to me, is true to one being inside the big spinning top of time. This top's velocity is two to three times the velocity of light* (372,000 to 558,000 miles per sound), *and we travel along with it and at the same time inside it.* Will we find it hard to believe we are going so fast, on the other hand, in such a short time? Therefore, our age of things, *and all things, even ourselves, are much older and in a very, very short interval, making us much older than we really are and can imagine.* At the same time, in a matter of seconds or split seconds with the big spinning top of time, relative to the velocity two to three times the velocity of light, *each second, as we know it, is not a second but two to three years, aging us and all things faster and, at the same time, in a much shorter time.* In reference to our calculating this movement by our measurement of things according to time as we know it or have it, *we, like the man in the space ship in outer space, trying to calculate his movement without object or movement of something relative to him, cannot and will not really calculate our movement in the big spinning top without relation to it.* We are inside it and at the same time moving with it unless we step outside the top of time, which is impossible because even if we could, where would we be? And that's where we would be, outside of time. *To what is time relative to? Since the man in the space ship is relative to the speed of light, and the speed of light is relative to a form of time, 186,000 miles per second, time itself is relative to what?* So, what is outside of time itself and to what is it relative? As Einstein's theory of special relativity states, all motion is relative. Hence, with the theory of relativity, we can never speak of absolute motion as such but only of motion relative to something else. In general, we cannot say that an object has the velocity of such and such, but that it has the velocity of such and such, relative to so and so—once again the theory of relativity. So with this in mind, it would be impossible for us to step outside of what I call the fourth dimension, time.

Referring back to Einstein's special theory of relativity, we can in some way apply this to the split-second theory of time in regard to our age, seasons, days, and nights, as we know them. In our age, like A and B in their rockets, relative to one another, with their relativity to the speed of light, 186,000 miles per second, you notice that if B, from the distance of A, was going at 93,000 miles per second, half the velocity of light, then B, on the other hand, as observed by A, seems to have shrunk. It has shrunk some three feet, as the book states, and as Einstein's theory shows. If they were separating at 161,000 miles per second, then to A, B's length would appear to be only ten feet. This is what's happening to us inside the vast big moving time top with the velocity two to three times that if light. *We are not shrinking, but instead aging quickly. Each second as we know it is not a second but, in reality, two to three years. In 1 minute, as we know it, we, in reality, would age 120-180 years.* We cannot see or notice this, and it would be hard for us to believe this or understand it. *But this is not impossible.* As the contraction theory shows, mass, with the increase of velocity, gets heavier, and at the same time, if velocitized at the speed of light, it would shrink. *Shrink into infinity.* Well, this same thing is happening to us in the time top, going at the velocity of two to three time the speed of light, aging us until *our shrinking becomes old age, and our infinity is none other than death itself.*

The seasons, as I have explained before, are not long intervals of months but quick flashes within seconds. (The velocity of time, 372,000 to 558,000 miles per second, compared to that of the speed of lights 186,000 miles per second, two to three times slower than the velocity of mass.)

The same holds true for our days and nights as with the seasons. They are the same as if you would click your home lightbulb on and off, as fast as you can, and you would get nothing but quick and short intervals of light and darkness. The same holds true with our days and nights, within seconds or split seconds and not twenty-four hour intervals as we know them.

So to what is time related? Nothing, only time itself, per se, and with everything else related to it. *Even the speed of light and Einstein's theory of $E = mc^2$, as shown in Faulkenstein's theory of $M = T = CG \div sec.$*

3

How and Why Newborn Babies Die

If we apply *Einstein's theory* of relativity and the velocity of light being 186,000 miles per second, and at the same time Faulkenstein's theory of M = T = CG ÷ sec., making the velocity of time two to three times the velocity of light, 372,000 to 558,000 miles per second, and then include *Charles Darwin's theory* of survival of the fittest by natural selection, we would find that the newborn baby, from one minute after delivery up until six weeks or six months and so on, being inside the top of time, with the velocity of 372,000 to 558,000 miles per second, *would have within 1 second, as we know it,* aged according to the seconds or time theory two to three years, and in one minute *the baby would have become 120-180 years old,* and so on. *In one day, the baby would have aged 172,800-259,000 years* but we, as youngsters or adults, having passed this age and lived, have proved, as Darwin's theory states, our survival to live because of our fitness at our time of birth by some unknown choosing of natural selection. Call it, if you like, a stronger form of health to have survived this crisis or even God's will, but some babies' bodies and chemical makeup are much weaker than others; some, not being able to withstand the time barrier, *at the same time age too fast* and die. The stronger, within this same time top, *do withstand this and live,* survive, and are among the many who at this very time are reading this page. Though this is hard to believe, the same holds true for us as we age thirty-five, forty-five, fifty-five, sixty-five and seventy-five years of age. Being inside the time theory, we are much older and, at the same time, weaker, and our systems break down for medical reasons, as we know them, and we, like the baby, are not able to withstand the time barrier, or as Darwin's theory states, *no longer fit to survive*, we therefore die.

Some Possible Answers to SIDS

The topic how and why newborn babies die, in my theory of $M = T = CG \div$ sec., is related strictly to SIDS, sudden infant, death syndrome, or crib death, this awful matter, which claims *15,000 to 20,000 newborn babies per year*. Also, this mysterious factor, according to my medical research, is as old as 4,000 years or so, but medical science has not come up with any cure or prevention. I would also venture to say that because of the lack of funds for research from the people and their government, all over the world, *SIDS has placed medical science in a dark age*, with very little hope for those innocent babies, if there continues to be very little change. However, there is some hope, if not an answer to this problem in Faulkenstein's theory, $M = T = CG \div$ sec. Also, I would venture to say that the answer or one of the answers has been under our noses for quite some time. Some of the answers to SIDS could be as follows:

1. The brain in many respects has shown in research, time after time, the great influence it has on the body and many times over the body. So, therefore, I suspect that *a recording device of the mother's heartbeat*, but some short time before delivery, of the child be played while the child sleeps during the age and stage of SIDS, one day to five months of age or at one day to six months. So while the child sleeps, the heartbeat on the tape will keep the brain of the child stimulated, and the brain in return will stimulate the body as well as the antibodies of the child, not allowing the antibodies to slow down to such a degree as to lead the body to such a degree of low activity that the whole system, both nervous and circulatory, would come to a sudden stop, resulting in death—a sudden life of activity passes on into the time

continuum; theologically this is a form of immortality. You see, what I think we overlook is that the child, while inside the body of the mother, long before delivery, is stimulated by the mother's heartbeat and other sounds. Therefore, the child is activated by the heartbeat of the mother as it continues to form. It has a surrounding that it's accustomed to. It has security, that when after delivery it slowly or quickly loses the stimulation it once had. It is no longer, or seldom, heard to stimulate or activate its antibodies. The whole body is slowed down until the baby cannot fend for itself because of lack of stimulation for the activation of antibodies. This results in death. However, *if the child's mind could be kept active while asleep,* that activation would be working as a stimulation to the body, and the body to the antibodies the child would be building up enough energy to fend for itself. *The reason why other babies never encounter SIDS is because they have either learned this process on their own or have kept a recording in their minds of the mother's heartbeat that continues to motivate them and stimulate them long after delivery.* Therefore, they are not subject to SIDS, or their body chemistry is much stronger to combat the celestial globe and has built up enough energy to withstand the same, therefore fulfilling a type like Darwin's survival of the fittest *by astronomical and cosmological selection,* by withstanding the time barrier of age three years every second, 180 years every minute, at the velocity of 558,000 miles per second.

2. The making of a recording of the mother's heartbeat a short time before delivery to be played while the child sleeps and while it awakes from time to time, *but it must be the heartbeat of that child's individual mother and no one else.*

3. To *devise a crib* with the sound and heartbeat of the mother. *When I said sound, I mean the noises of the mother's insides that the child would be accustomed to hearing if still inside the body of the mother, along with the heartbeat. This crib could be used while the child sleeps, picking up the vibrations that it has grown accustomed to.* This crib would place the child right back in that state of sleep after stimulization, activation, and motivation of its body cells and antibodies. This, in return, would

24

be building up energy in the body over a period of time to enable the child to get through the SIDS stage and later fend for itself. This is the same as an average adult who, when tired, has no energy. So while in this state the body runs down or is running down, but once rested, feels refreshed with energy and vigor restored. The SIDS child is the same way. *So what is the SIDS child, you might ask, tired from?* Well the SIDS child uses up its energy while awake, playing and exploring; this may seem like nothing at all to the adult, *but it is a great exertion for the child.* Then, while the child sleeps, the body has no outside force as it does when awake, and therefore the cells receive very little stimulation, activation, and motivation *like the great activity of the brain of the adult.* The body slows down more because it was already run down; with no stimuli it comes to a complete stop, with the child resting on forever.

4. The SIDS child's body, but not necessarily the system, is run down; that is *why in many cases you will find that it sleeps more and harder. Also, when awake, it may or may not play harder or longer. Therefore, when asleep, it needs something to stimulate it back to the procedure of energic restoration.* The process the SIDS child goes through in this state of body worriness is like an average person having a dream that they are falling off a boat, train, car mountain, etc., but *before that person hits bottom, he wakes up or jumps up and says, "What a dream,"* but then what would happen *if that person didn't wake up? It is possible* he could die in his sleep. Well, that's what happens to the SIDS child; the child does not have these bad dreams, *but the child is in such a state close to this* that its little body cannot generate or regenerate enough energy to restore itself to strength and vigor, and it dies. The person or persons who find the SIDS child no longer alive think that what is happening is a bad dream.

(Please note that the SIDS theory is on file in the law office of Daniel L. Twer, associate of Morris, James, Hitchens & Williams, Market Street Tower, Wilmington, Delaware: pp. 25, 25a, 25b, 25c; under its original title $M = T = CG \div sec.$; under the protection of United States Common Law copyright for unpublished works December 20, 1972.)

4

The Pseudoscientific Metaphysical Cause and Effect of Progeria or Alzheimer Disease

Progeria, Alzheimer Disease, Pick's Disease, and Werner's Syndrome have five things in common, though they have some fair, or good degree of difference between them. But the five things that they all have in common are:
1. Premature aging
2. Sclerodermalike changes
3. Graying hair
4. Baldness
5. Leg ulcers
And within the field of modern medicine, all of them are categorized under "Disorders of the Nervous System and Behavior" and classified within the field or topic of "'dementia." But, by the same token, these diseases are not by pure biomedical rights the disease (progeria) per se. Alzheimer Disease, Pick's Disease, and Werner's Syndrome are most prominently found in young adults twenty-five to forty years of age. At times they appear in some even younger or older than twenty-five to forty and, therefore, medically speaking Werner's Syndrome is also called or known as adult progeria. What I'm concerned with is child progeria or childhood progeria, which strikes one out of eight million children and which causes the child to age prematurely

at a rate of eight to ten years faster than the natural or average child. The physical effect are:
1. Premature aging
2. Sclerodermalike changes
3. Graying hair
4. Baldness
5. Leg ulcers
6. Arthritis
7. Change in voice tone
8. Dwarflike height
9. Diminutive body frame
10. A much lower degree of dementia or hardly any dementia, because many of these children are A or B students and very much alert.

Therefore, childhood progeria is in many ways different from the other progerias. Also it should be pointed out that modern medicine gives very little explanation as to why this disease occurs or how, when, and who is subject to it. Nor can it be predetected or prevented, and, to date, there is no cure. Very little can be done in regard to treatment. Most important of all, more is known about the adult progeria than the child progeria. Therefore, I would like to attempt to give an explanation of both adult and childhood progeria by way of my theory of meta-physicotheologocosmologingology, in which I feel that I have found the answer and explanation, which I term the *pseudo-scientific metaphysical cause and effect of progeria.*

Part One—Adult Progeria

I feel that the adult progeria is nothing more than the pseudo-scentific metaphysical cause and effect of the theory of $M = T = C.G. \div$ by seconds. Mass equals time equals, a Celestial Globe divided by seconds. The time factor and element, based upon the light velocity of 186,000 miles per second, and the time velocity being two or three times faster than light, makes the time velocity 372,000 to 558,000 miles per second, which in turn is aging everything and all matter two or three years a second, and in just one minute 120 to 180 years old, and in just one twenty-four-hour-day—172,800 to 259,000 years old.

This technically is the space time, or celestial time in which all processes are aging in our universe, astrometaphysically, or celestralphysically. *But then the pseudoscientific metaphysical cause and effect is Terrestrially viewed, or seen as a aging process of eight to ten years more than average or normal.* Thus the side effects are rapid or premature aging. Thus if a person is thirty-five years old, then metaphysically or pseudoscientifically metaphysically speaking, he is 350 to 385 years older. And the eight to ten years' difference depends on their time velocity factor. In other words, are they in the time continum of the second or third time element, of 372,000 or 558,000 M.P.C.? *If their celestial time element is 372,000 M.P.C. then their Terrestrial aging process would be eight years as we know it. And if they're in the third element, then their aging process would be ten years as we know it.* Thus the age of thirty-five in the second time element equals 280 years plus 35 equals 315 years old. There are some who wish to exclude the additional thirty-five years, thus making the said person only 280 years old. But I choose to add their additional thirty-five years due to the fact that I feel it too should be taken into account because it is a part of their age. But by the same token, celestially a person is 172,800 to 259,000 years old by the day as we know it. Therefore, on the Terrestrial plane it shouldn't be too hard for us to understand the aging process of the adult progerian, though one may find it hard to believe. And this too shouldn't be too hard, if we keep an open mind about this matter and study again and again Faulkenstein's pseudoscientific metaphysical cause and effect of progeria or Alzheimer disease.

Part Two—Childhood Progeria

I cannot help but feel that childhood progeria has a close link with SIDS (Sudden Infant Death Syndrome). And my reason for saying this is because of the reverse process that has taken place between the two classes of children. The SIDS child's lifespan is short, and, if I may say so, all too short. But the progeria child's lifespan is exceptionally long, that is, long pseudoscientifically metaphysically speaking. I cannot help but think, and deeply feel, that the progeria child is none other than the SIDS child growing up, or transferred. In chapter 3, "How and Why

28

Newborn Babies Die," I stated that, if we apply Einstein's theory of relativity, the velocity of light being 186,000 miles per second, and at the same time Faulkenstein's theory of $M = T = C.G. \div$ by seconds making the velocity of time two or three times the velocity of light, 372,000 to 558,000 miles per second, and then include Charles Darwin's Theory of survival of the fittest by natural selection, we would find that the newborn baby inside the top of time with the velocity of 372,000 to 558,000 miles per second would have, within one second as we know it, aged accordingly to the seconds, or time theory two or three years, and in one minute the baby would have become 120 to 180 years old. And so on. And in one day, the baby would have aged 172,800 to 259,000 years. But we as youngster or adults have passed this age and lived and proved Darwin's theory survival to live because of our fitness at our time of birth by some unknown process of natural selection. But some babies' bodies and chemical make-up are much weaker than others and unable to withstand the time barrier, at the same time they age too fast and die, while the more stronger within this same time do withstand this and live. And all of this leaves me to conclude, or suspect that the survival, or survivors of this time factor are divided into three parts. The first survivors live and go through a normal, natural, healthy lifespan (meaning the average human being growing old and dying naturally).

The second survivors are pre-progerians. These pre-progerians are those who suffer from childhood progeria. And the third survivors are the post-progerians, meaning those who suffer from adult progeria. But these pre-progerians miraculously escape their crib death, but not the time-element aging factor and thus transferred rapid aging eight to ten years more than normal, resulting in progeria. But once again we must rely on the time velocity factor of the second or third time element. *Then if they are in the second time element, we must add eight years to their natural, or present age, and ten years must be added if they are in the third time element.* Thus if the child is ten years old, then by progeria or pseudoscientific metaphysical methods he would be 100 years old, or 110, because we are counting ten years plus one, or one year plus ten. *We must not overlook their natural giving years.* Then in the third time element *if a child is eight years old they are 80 + 8 = 88, because we include each year also.* Likewise for post-progeria. If they are thirty-five natural years old, then pseudoscientifically metaphysically speaking and in the third time element they are 350 years, plus, 35, equalling 385 years. Nor is this a far-fetched figure due to the fact that there are people who reach their natural hundredth birthdays.

So, if we keep an open mind about Faulkenstein's pseudo-scientific metaphysical cause and effects of progeria, none of this is too hard to understand or believe. Also, we may ask the question "How do we know when a person is in the time element of the second or third velocity?" *On the 8th or 10th year factor?* While I would think the best way to tell the difference would be to check and compare one diseased person to the other, I'm sure that in both cases of the disease, progeria or childhood progeria, there are cases in which rapid aging is more prominent in one compared to the other. And the physical signs are more noticeable. Also, I am sure we can ask why adult progeria, or as I label it, post-progeria appears at the age of thirty-five to forty? My answer to this is that at this age period, biomedically, biochemically, and biophysically speaking, *the human body starts to begin its regressive processes in which we term the "change of life."* Though this may seem premature to most of us, this is precisely the point, and a case in point. And the term "premature" in these special cases results in rapid aging, thus progeria, or post-progeria, and, medically speaking, Werner's Syndrome, Pick's Disease, or Alzheimer Disease. Also we can ask why this doesn't happen to all of us? And my answer or explanation is that once again the universal pseudoscientific metaphysical law of survival of the fittest by natural selection comes into play here. We who are more mentally and physically fit bypass this crisis and disease. But those who are the opposite fall prey, or become victim to adult or post-progeria. It is also my belief that these adult progerians and childhood progerians grow up to be transferred to a later time and age period of thirty-five to forty when the body's chemical and physical magnetism and metabolism is most weak or vulnerable during its medical-evolutional change of life, such as the female menopause and the male climacteric. So once again I feel safe in saying that if we look into this matter of progeria, both childhood and adult, or, as I labeled them pre-progeria or post-progeria, with an open mind, there is no sensible and intelligent reason not to view the SIDS child as the progeria child transferred or growing up and the progeria adult as the progeria child delayed or bypassed until the age of thirty to forty, when the delayed process is matured, and the bypass unavoidable.

5

Some Comments on God, Space, and Time

God, God to man, in an educated or metaphysical sense, is as big in imagination and thought as space and time. The truth of it all is that we know very little of the three but pride ourselves in our belief in knowing what we really, in fact, fall short of factually knowing. We believe in what we have first been taught, trained, reared, or conditioned in one way or another to believe, be it from the fields of divinity, theology, philosophy, liberal arts, and science, *but, in reality, are they all the truth? Are any of them true?* For we have been told as well as taught that God doesn't have a beginning. Well, to me, this belief or teaching is *metaphysically false, for I believe God has a beginning.* The truth is we as mere men don't know that beginning only He does. Everything that has a beginning has an ending. This may be so, but when applied to God, He will never end due to the fact that this applies to all things material and natural. *Since God is nonmaterial and supernatural, the laws of physics do not apply, but metaphysicis does.* In this sense, we would find it impossible for God to have had a beginning but at the same time no end. This would not be hard for us to believe or understand due to the fact that we, while living, know of our condition of life but know nothing directly of death. *For in order to know directly, we must first die.* So, in a sense, God can be looked at in this view. Since we really don't know God's beginning, we follow by saying He has no ending and fulfill the Scriptures in the statement that He was and always will be. *Second to this, God, knowing his beginning, doesn't sell himself short in any way; we would sell ourselves in knowing our date of birth.* We, being natural and physical, know that sooner or later we must die. But God is unnatural compared to man, supernatural and non-physical, spiritual and metaphysical. Therefore, the element of death is not in Him but only in the mind of men. This could be the meaning of a book entitled *Is God Dead?*

1. Space? There is no such thing as space. If we apply the $M = T = CG \div$ sec. theory, then it would be and has been wrong for us to believe in such a thing, as space. Scientists and thinkers, over the ages, such as Augustine, Aquinas, Dante, Timaeus, Descartes, Aristotle, Berkeley, Gilber, Faraday, Plato, Einstein, and many others, have argued on the meaning of space and varied in their opinion. The opinion as to whether it is infinite or finite, vacuum or not, void or empty. *First, there is much controversy as to what space is for in the scape as space. I would say there is no space but place.* For we measure space by numerical forms and words. However, it would be better if we concentrated on thought. For I believe all that we call space is occupied with object or matter, seen or unseen to us, *and because we cannot see or observe a thing doesn't mean it doesn't exist.* We can't see all the planets either that occupy space, as we know it, or see an electron; nonetheless, science tells us they exist. If we were to use a simple form of Einstein's theory of relativity, all things are relative to something, then the same would apply to space, having it occupied by something though invisible. *This invisible space is not space but place; place of distance between one thing and another.* You see, words are confusing, here and at play and also in the time theory of Mass $= T = CG \div$ sec. *There is no such thing as outer space:* Out of one place or into another, but this is not outer space. *For the time theory* shows us that *we are inside a big spinning top* going at the velocity of two to three times the velocity of light, 186,000

miles per second. So we are in a top going 372,000 to 558,000 miles per second and everything that exists is inside of it. *Outside of it there is nothing.* For all that is and would or could be is inside the TOP, and *the only way to go into outer space as we would know it is to go outside the time top,* which is impossible. So, while inside the top, we very easily see it as big, high and vast into outer space. But while inside the top of time and never able to go outside of it while on the earth, which is like a speck inside the Time Globe, we are like a speck on earth, compared to the solar system, which is like a speck compared to the whole universe, known and unknown to us, which is like a speck compared to the Big Spinning Top of Time. *When we leave the ground or earth, we call it outer space, but this is not true. For the truth is that we are in outer place, in another place. We are still inside the top.* To equal our belief of outer space, we must go outside of a 372,000-558,000 miles per second spinning top. This is really outer space *provided there is space outside of it.*

So you see, while *in a big circle, to a man who stands on earth* and looks out, the solar system looks big to him. Now if he would go to an outer place from the earth and stand on the moon, inside the solar system, then the whole universe would look big to him, yet he is inside the spinning top of time. *If he would venture out of it, the whole universe would look small to him, you see?* So unless and until man can venture outside the big time Celestial globe, with the velocity of 372,000 to 558,000 miles per second, then *there can never be any real outer space.* And as long as he remains inside the top and ventures from the earth to the moon or other planets, then he is only in outer place. So educators, scientists, and universities or colleges should cease the study of outer space and begin the new study of outer place.

2. Time? Time, as I have already stated, is a thing that measures all things, but at the same time all things can't measure it. Time is not a vastness or an ocean of space and nothingness but a complete circle believed to be unmeasurable. But, if measurable, then, as I have stated before, I would apply to the highest numerical digit known to us, which would place it somewhere in the decillion of miles. Though as vast and big as this circle

may be, it is, as I believe Einstein said, along with many other scientists, *a continuum*. This would imply that it is, in this fashion, infinity, therefore having no end.

With this in mind, I am inclined to believe, as others, that it is no doubt, *the fourth dimension*. Anything else that I or anyone else would try to in any way add or take away is mere speculation and, therefore, in the laws of physics, metaphysics, or metaphysicotheologocosmologingology, would have no foundation to support their logic.

As I have stated before, time with its vastness of miles, as the circumference in a circle, also has a velocity, and that velocity is two to three times faster than the speed of light. And I base my assumption on the fact that science has shown us that sound traveling in substance has seven velocities; they are:

Substance	Speed: ft./sec.
Air	1,126
Hydrogen	4,315
Carbon dioxide	877
Water	4,820
Iron (steel)	16,800
Brass	11,500
Granite	12,960

Second to this is the speed of light, 186,000 miles per second, and *since sound and light are both objects of time*, both at the same time traveling inside time, with light of the two being the highest velocity then it is only natural, unbelievable common sense, and imaginative that time should be faster and has its own natural velocity of 372,000 to 558,000 miles per second, though it may seem to us unbelievable. *And as the same holds true that we have no instrument to measure the speed of light, to prove its unbelievable speed, but yet believe it, then the same should hold true that we have no instrument in which to measure time,* but a broad enough mind to imagine it. Though, in time, I believe we will have ships to travel the speed, or near the speed, of light, in so doing, we will say that we have broken the time barrier, but this will not be so due to the fact that every object in existence, known and unknown to us in the theory of M = T ÷ CG = sec., shows *us that we already have.* And though we achieve in space ships of the future the velocity of light, still this would be secondary because M = T = CG ÷ sec. *shows us that time and not light is the main factor.*

As to how time could be a complete circle as an elliptical shape Einstein showed that light in the universe, when it travels through the universe, not in a straight line but a type-like straight line. *But with the universe being elliptical, light would travel from a given point and then back again.* So if the universe is round or elliptical and light travels from one point and back again, then *it is only natural that this with light and the universe inside it* would naturally be a circle or elliptical in shape.

In the book Relativity for the Layman, it states that an airplane moving at a rate of 750 miles an hour relative to an observer *would shrink by about a millionth of a millionth of an inch* or about the diameter of the nucleus. Such small amounts are not even detectible with our most precise instruments, *let alone being noticed by the human eye.* So I could say in relation to this that the same holds true with our not being able to notice how fast time is moving and our not moving with it, but inside it. *Nor can we notice how fast we are aging, or seasons change.* Our days and nights with the seasons all in a flash then repeat themselves in a flash and so on. *Nor, do we have any scientific instruments to show us the vastness of movement.* So this, too, would also make it harder for us to accept or believe we are moving inside a big spinning top called time, going at a velocity of 372,000 to 558,000 miles per second, two to three times the velocity of light, which is 186,000 miles per second.

The special theory of relativity, in its reference to mass increase, states that if two men, A and B, had a mass of 1,000 pounds when at rest with respect to one another and if A measures B's mass while they are moving, relative to each other, he would find that B's mass appears to have increased its numerical value. If A and B both have a rest mass of 1,000 pounds, each when at rest

36

respective to each other on earth, *then, when approaching or separating at a relative velocity of 93,000 miles per second,* B would appear to have a mass of about 1,200 pounds if A measured B's mass by attempting to stop him or by some other, similar method. *At 161,000 miles per second,* B's mass would be 2,000 pounds *or twice as great, and at higher velocity* B's mass would be even greater, if B would measure A's mass, the same thing would apply. Then when they are at rest, the two men's mass would revert back to 1,000 pounds.

So the mass equation increase states that when an object is moving with respect to an observer, the mass of the object becomes greater. The amount of increase depends on the relative velocity of object and observer. In this case, it is ironic that some people attempt to decrease their mass with vigorous exercise, often by running, when the special theory of relativity says that their mass will increase. *The faster they run, the greater their mass because;* for example, if a 300-pound man runs fifteen miles an hour, his mass will increase by about a millionth of a millionth of an ounce (000,000,000,001). *However, the effect would be greater if he could run faster. The reader is cautioned against believing that the mass increase effect means an object becomes bigger in the sense of its physical dimensions, width, length, and height, for this is not true. You can visualize an object becoming heavier without it becoming larger,* and keep in mind that the contraction effect predicts that it actually becomes smaller in size, while its mass increases when moving relative to the observer. This I hold true, *for in the big spinning top material things remain the same to our eyes though they are moving in time at the velocity of 372,000 to 558,000 miles per second.* Second, we in the spinning top, at the velocity of 372,000 to 558,000 miles per second, *using the contraction theory,* will find that though we are moving two to three times the speed of light, *we get no bigger but at the same time get older.* As we can visualize in the special theory of relativity, an object becoming heavier without it becoming larger, *according to Einstein's theory of $E = mc^2$,* we should not find it hard to visualize that with *Faulkenstein's theory of $M = T = CG \div sec.$,* we are going at a velocity of

372,000-558,000 miles per second and do not change physically in length, width, or height. Using the contraction theory, we do at the same time get older instead of smaller, and it is on this point of Einstein's theory of two-twin brothers who if one of them, we shot into outer space in a rocket at the velocity of light (186,000) miles per second and the other brother was left on earth, *the brother in the rocket would be much younger than his brother on earth when he returns. This I do not agree with.* Mass = time = celestial globe ÷ sec. shows us, first of all, that by being inside the 372,000-558,000 miles per second time capsule, *we automatically age 120 to 180 years on a material basis.* So for one on a more higher base, motivated by an instrument, at the velocity of 186,000 miles per second, adding to his natural age, 558,000 to 726,000 personal, *meaning time capsule movements, plus the rockets 726,000, he would be much older,* whereas his brother on the ground naturally, with the speed of time 558,000 miles per second, (three times the speed of light) each individual second equalling 3-years. *In 60 seconds, as we know it, he would be 180 years old; the other brother has the natural velocity of time 558,000, plus the rocket, 186,000; he in 60 seconds would be 240 years old, compared to his brother, 180 years old. Sixty years older.* Then, again, we could say *by taking the rocket with the brother in it out of one time barrier of 558,000 or 372,000 and placing him in another one less 372,000 to 186,000, yes, according to Einstein he would be younger, while the brother on earth would be older by some sixty years.* However, we must keep in mind that the rocket is still inside the time capsule and not outside of it, and we have already shown that there is no such thing as outer space but outer place. So the brother in the rocket, motivated by another form, is still caught up inside the spinning top with its time plus the rocket's motivated time, and we should see that still he would be older by sixty years.

Now once again, science tells us that *nothing can travel faster than the speed of light* because we have seen with the *contraction theory*, plus the speed of light, that *not only does the object's length shrink into nothing, but its mass becomes infinite or disappears. However, Faulkenstein's theory* shows that this may be true but not with time. For, in a way, this is what time consists of. For mass in the time's theory is not there, or a material object, as we know it, or the body of a thing, *but mass in the time's theory is really space as we know it. Space in the theory is a place or places, and place or places are in themselves in time, the spinning top, the fourth dimension.* What has happened is that unmaterial or nonmaterialized massless substance, by its own laws, unknown to us, produced a vast big spinning top that engulfed all things in existence into it. While spinning at 558,000-372,000 miles per second, it spilled an ocean of stillness within it that we call space, and when looking out into it from the earth, we think of a quiet stillness, called infinity. *Any material object that is shot out into it, with a part of time's velocity* (186,000 miles per second), *would become a part of this infinity and shrink into nothingness.* It is in this that we do have something faster than the speed of light to which the speed of light is relative, and that is the speed of time, the fourth dimension, with light traveling inside it. James A. Coleman states in *Relativity for the Layman,* that the reader is cautioned against concluding that time is an additional physical dimension in the sense that it can be seen and felt like a material object. *For no one in our universe can see in four dimensions or more because of the way our universe is constructed.* He also goes on to mention that time appears slower on the other's system to two observers traveling with a constant velocity relative to each. This has given rise to the famous time clock paradox. To illustrate, *we must first make clear that when time appears slower on a moving system, not only do the clocks on that system appear slower, but all time processors are slowed down. This means that digestive processes, biological processes, atomic activity, are all slowed down.*

With this in mind, then the clock paradox is stated as follows: a rocket ship, manned by several men, is all set for a space trip to Arcturus in the constellation Bootes, the Herdsman, which is thirty-three light years from the earth. If the rocket travels at a velocity close to the velocity of light, it will arrive on Arcturus a little over thirty-three years later, earth time. And if it returns immediately, it will arrive back on earth about sixty-six years after leaving the earth.

Since the rocket has been moving with a high velocity relative to the earth, *all time processes in the rocket have been slowed down considerably. It will not seem to the men on the rocket that it took thirty-three years to make the one-way trip.* In all probability, they will be pulling into the region of Arcturus just about the time they get gurgles in their stomachs to tell them they're hungry. And when they arrive back on earth, it will seem to them that only a day has elapsed. But to the people on earth, it will have been sixty-six years. When the men alight from the rocket, they will find that their wives, who were young when they left them, are now too old and feeble to come and meet them, or still worse, that they have long since died of old age! And some of the men might even be faced with the startling prospect of having to greet a hitherto unknown son or daughter who is sixty-six years older than they! It might seem enticing to keep young by traveling about in space, but it does have its complications!

But this isn't all. We found from the first postulate that all motion is relative, so we can really view the space trip as *if the rocket stood still but the earth went off* in the opposite direction on a voyage through space and back. *The theory now says that the time processes on earth will be slowed down relative to those in the rocket. Hence, when the earth returns to the rocket sixty-six years later, everyone on earth will be but a day older, while the men on the rocket will be sixty-six years older!* From this point of view, the young wives and children will now find themselves with old men for husbands and fathers!

This is a paradox: At the end of such a rocket trip, will the people on the earth be older than the people in the rocket, or will the rocket people be older than the people on earth? *Both views appear to be correct according to the special theory. Yet they are contradictory, and both cannot be true.*

With the advent of rocket research in recent years and its use in space travel in the foreseeable future, considerable interest in this clock paradox has been regeneratd. Not only has the paradox been seriously debated in scientific journals, but many people are claiming, in all seriousness, that *people who continually engage in space travel will remain perpetually young. This is not true as the following explanation of the apparent paradox will show.*

Although the special theory does predict a slowing down of the time processes when two observers are moving relative to each other, it applies only when their relative velocity is constant. It does not apply in the case of a rocket *taking off from the earth and later landing because in the launching and landing processes, the rocket is accelerating and decelerating,* i.e., *its velocity is not constant. Here, the general theory would apply, and it has been shown that the slowing down of the time processes* that occurs in the rocket when, after takeoff, it is *moving with constant velocity relative to the earth is cancelled out when the rocket's velocity is changing during launching and landing.* Hence, *there is no permanent effect* and, of course, no paradox.

It might be argued by some that *if a rocket* (or *some type of space platform*), *once it has been launched,* were *to circle the earth continually at the same speed without ever landing again, the effect would in this case be permanent, and the fountain of youth would be attained.* This reasoning is fallacious, however, because a rocket circling our planet with constant speed is not traveling with constant velocity. *Constant velocity means that the speed and direction are constant. Here, in order to keep the rocket moving in a circle,* a force must be applied that results in an acceleration, and the special theory and its predictions would not apply.

So Einstein's special theory of relativity does contradict itself and in some cases could not factually apply. But *Faulkenstein's theory* of Mass = time = celestial globe ÷ sec. could show us a better age difference. First, Einstein's theory is in some ways dealing with the difference of age between the man in the rocket ship and the people on earth; then other parts of his theory are contradictory. *Also, the special theory and its predictions do not apply because his whole theory is mostly rested to the ve-*

41

*locity of light and the earth relative to it. Faulkenstein's theory
of time and seconds revolves not just around the speed of light,
but at the same time, the speed of time,* such as: (1) the speed
of time; (2) the speed of light inside time; (3) the rocket relative to the speed of light and time; and (4) the people on earth.

Now as the seconds theory of time has already shown, the
speed of time is two to three times faster than the speed of light
(372,000 to 558,000 miles per second). This time matter is a big
spinning top with the speed of light and the earth and the solar
system and the cosmos and everything in existence, as well, inside it. With this in mind, *we have already stated before that we
are naturally according to how fast the spinning top is going.*
If it is going twice the velocity of light, 372,000 miles per second,
then each second known to us would equal two years. Then, in
sixty seconds, we would be 120 years old. If the time top is going
three times the velocity of light, then each second would equal
three years, and in sixty seconds we would be 180 years old. Now
let's say that Einstein's men are in the space ship, moving inside
the spinning top, with the top going twice the speed of light,
372,000 miles per second. The men in the space ship leaving earth,
while the ship is going only the speed of light, 186,000 miles per
second, no matter how far they would go out and come back,
would be sixty years in difference. *If it took them in the book,*
Relativity for the Layman, *33 years to go to the nearest planet
and 33 years to come back, they would still be sixty or sixty-six
years older.* The reason for this is that the *people on earth, with
their natural time barrier of 372,000 miles per second,* would remain the same in age. The men in the rocket because they are
moving with the rocket's time barrier, of *186,000 miles* per second with the rocket still inside the spinning top, with the top
going still 372,000 miles per second, *so the speed of the rocket
plus the time would age the men in the rocket sixty years older;
the people on earth, naturally moving with the time top would
be sixty years younger.* But *if the spinning top velocity were
three times the speed of light, 558,000 miles per second, the men
in the rocket still doing 186,000 miles per second, then the people
on the earth would be older, while the men in the rockets would*

42

be sixty years younger. The people on earth would have in the time top superseded the men in the rocket three times their velocity. Although the rocket is inside the top of time, *still the people on earth have a jump on the rocket by velocity, and this would in nowise effect the rocket any. The only thing to change this is for the rocket to jump from 186,000 to 372,000 miles per second.* But if the rocket did this, then the rocket would be 372,000 plus 186,000 extra. The earth would be doing the velocity of the men in the rocket, so the earth would be going at a velocity of 558,000 miles per second. *What, then, about their age?* It would appear that they would be the same, but they wouldn't. The men in the rocket increasing their velocity at the same time increase their age. But then, too, wouldn't this make them by now the age of the people on earth? No, because the people on earth would still have their sixty previous year's jump. This is how Faulkenstein's theory differs from that of Einstein's.

6

Gravity in the Top

Gravity in this vast and big spinning top is the same as that which Newton and Einstein considered. However, Faulkenstein's gravitation and winds in the time theory would be as follows: first, we must picture the whole universe and cosmos with solar systems all within this spinning top just going at the velocity of 372,000-558,000 miles per second. With this in mind, we know that this would keep all the planets, stars, and other objects in their place. Second, only if the top stops would the earth, planets, stars, and ourselves be thrown out of place. Third, we can now go on to imagine that the whole universe, with its solar systems and cosmos, is round but big, spinning and at the same time finite and unbounded, as Einstein states. *Fourth, it is round or elliptical, in the radius, not two hundred sextillion as Einstein states* (200,000,000,000,000,000,000,000) *but instead two hundred decillion* (200,000,000,000,000,000,000,000,000,000,000,000). Now, with all of this in mind, we are now ready to commit it to gravitation inside it.

Now the gravitation in the top of time can be considered in this manner. Take, a basin of water, with the basin being round, of course, and spin the water around and around. As you spin the water, you will notice circles forming in ring-type shapes. Now this basin, let's say is twenty-four inches in diameter. You would notice at least six to eight rings forming in the basin, *which in the spinning top of time, would constitute the spheres of our universe. The bigger the basin, the more rings. So, the same applies to our two hundred decillion universe or top with the stars, planets, moon,* and *sun that we do know like those basin rings, riding on them, each to their own ring. Without your noticing it, these rings, while moving, are giving off a form of vibration,* like air, but the water would have to be moving at a high velocity for you to feel it. Nonetheless, it is doing so, and this is what's taking place inside the universe. Since the time theory shows us that the spinning top we are in has the velocity of 372,000-558,000 miles per second, we feel this air of the water basin and in this way we have our gravity. Now the same air inside the top, which is round and bounded, is circling through these rings and at the same time from them. Before going any further, *I would like to point out that as the water in the basin spins faster and faster, you will notice that it rises higher and higher, thus making our universe rings to us farther and farther out into what we call space.* Now the air in this top flowing through would bounce off or to and fro in the top, and as we would have objects or people in the top with their own distance from one another, they would feel this air at different times. Therefore, as if they were in a polygon, this air would be like to us north, east, south, and west winds. Now let's turn back to the gravity of it all. *We, like the object in a basin of water, are riding on rings, which science would call orbit or axis.* Let's imagine that a star that burns out, such as a comet that's been thrown off its rings, in the *vicinity of Pluto, the most outer known planet, some 3,670,000,000 miles from the sun, the eighth planet.* Out of the hundred of rings, let's say that Pluto's ring is the eighth one known to us. As this comet is falling through the rings, with its force and velocity, *the comet would not ride the other rings. Instead, it would be like a pebble skimming on the water, jumping from one ring to another; then it would reach the last ring which would be earth. When comets enter our atmosphere, about sixty-five miles above the earth's surface, they began to glow and we see them; than later they crash.* This example holds true for both meteorite, and comets. Science tells us that at one time it was thought that the appearance of a comet was entirely unpredictable, but many comets are regular visitors. They are, in fact, part of our solar system, like the planets they orbit the sun, but unlike the planets, their orbits are highly ellipitical, which, in this theory, would make them a circle, like the water in the basin. Now if we drop an object on one of the rings in the basin, we will soon see that the object returns to the dropping point. So, in this same way, we see in the spinning top the returning of the comets. A comet goes around the sun, science tells us, and then starts back on its long journey through the solar system. Like the rings in a basin I have already pointed out, so, too, in our spinning top of 372,000-558,000 miles per second with its hundreds of rings. Enckes' comet will be back again in about 3.3 years, it has the shortest period of any known comet. Since it was first discovered in 1786, not a single return has been missed, though the comet can be seen only with the aid of a telescope. The most famous of all comets, Halley's, has a period of about seventy-six years, it was last seen in 1910, and it is expected to return in 1986. So as to all things in the top, holding its own parts and not venturing from it, we know that sometimes, even inside the top, that some things can turn so fast that, like the basin of water, they can be sucked in or thrown out of place into another, from one ring in the top, called spheres, orbit, and axis, to another, though at the same time nonstopping. *Also, I believe these rings to go on spinning for billions and billions of years at a time.*

7

The Split-Second Theory

In the book entitled *Albert Einstein, the Man and His Theories,* Hilaire Cuny, on page 21, says that the stars we see and observe are not the exact same ones we see each night, but different ones, because of the constant movement of the universe. *We can not be certain that these same stars exist, today, earth time, when we look at them, but only that they existed there more than 4, 11, 30, 50, or 100 years ago.* If we use a powerful telescope or a radio telescope to observe them, we are capturing the invisible wave lengths they transmitted thousands, million, hundred of millions, or even eleven billion years ago. *So even if a person took a snapshot of a star, the picture wouldn't even be good for that moment because what he has actually taken is a picture of a star that has long disappeared, and others may have been born thousands of years ago without our realizing it.* So that's what's happening inside the spinning top of time. Like the stars, we, too, the people on the earth inside this same time clock, are aging so fast, about 120 to 180 years per sixty seconds, that we don't even realize it.

Man, in the split-second theory, could be like the Einstein conception. However, I would venture to say that mass, and all mass as we know it, would not necessarily become infinite, increased in terms of its velocity, when a given motion reaches the speed of light. *However, I would say that the spinning top with*

47

all mass inside it, every kind of mass, is spinning at 372,000-558,000 miles per second, until what has happened is that everything has frozen. Frozen stiff, as to keep all material, objects, matter, and mass whole, whole, whatever its physical makeup. The active atoms are kept together because everything is frozen *—not a cool type of frozen but like a stillness.* Everything is moving so fast that we are in a stillness, which keeps everything with its own individual makeup together. *If the spinning top that we're in would stop, we would crumble like dust, as would everything else in existence. So when we take an object of any kind and shoot it at the velocity of light, 186,000 per second,* one to two times less the speed or velocity of the spinning top of time, then—quite true—we're taking an object from one point of time and reducing it to another slower time—at the same time quite fast *but not fast enough to keep its physical form. Therefore, it is reduced to dust, and we call it infinite because of the fact that we can't see it or its form as we knew it.*

So it's not the velocity of light or the increase of an object to the velocity of light that would in return make an object infinite but the decrease of velocity of the time top that gives everything or enables everything to hold its form. *When the velocity of the time top with relation to an object is decreased from 372,000 to 558,000 miles per second down to 186,000 miles per second, the object loses form and we call this disappearing infinity.* The last writings of this theory will deal with the following:

1. How, where, when, and why was the universe created?
2. Who created it?
3. How the spinning top came to be?
4. What spins the spinning top?

When I say that we are turning so fast that we are in a frozen state of stillness, I mean that we have this frozen stillness, not the cool cold frozenness that we know *but a state of being spun so fast until every atom, mass, and matter of objects keeps their form and whole mass, and while we remain in this state, we see everything in its full and wholeness. But if the time capsule stopped,* then we and everything would lose our form and cease to exist. But as we continue along in this capsule of time, the fourth dimension, though in a frozen stillness, we and also all things have flexibility, which empowers us or things to move on their own. Such as we are on the earth, and the earth is rotating on its axis, and we are turning with the earth. But, at the same time, we have our flexibility to move up and down in it, from side to side in it, or back and forth in it, and travel north, east, south, and west in it. This would give us a type like four corners of the earth, with 90 degree angles, (4 x 90 = 360); this brings us back when traveling to our staring point. It shows us that we can travel around the world but in a circle. This is what I mean by flexibility. *We have this flexibility, though traveling in the time top 372,000 to 558,000 miles per second, though riding in a state of stillness,* thus keeping our form of self and things.

8

How the Universe Was Created

I must start off by trying to answer these questions with the old philosophical proverb that for every reason, there is a cause. For nothing is of itself without cause and the reason for it. For every action, there is a reaction.

Our universe was created through an action triggered by a reaction and a reaction causing a chain of reactions. This action could be the same one that the theorist Canon Lemaitne once spoke of. His theory visualizes the original assemblage of the matter, all matter and energy of the whole universe in one body. *A single superatom. So Faulkenstein goes on to say that with all this activity, causing and recausing many actions, one action splits into another, causing it to form an action.* At the same time, the universe was in its birth to form what would later be to us a fixed, still, and quiet universe, out of all or once a chaotic catastrophe. *This superatom, at the same time, was very compact with stars close together and galaxies very recently made, and at the same time in the making with collisions and explosions often happening.* Then from all this, masses of flying gases, in the heat of space and time, *whatever space and time was then, liquid or solid,* cooled into planetlike bodies, with a wide range of sizes. Then shattering and exploding bodies produced dust grain and gases from which later stars were born.

When was the universe created? I would venture to say some ten to fifteen billion years ago. However, there may be some doubt about this to some people, but people are accustomed to doubt, aren't they?

Where was the universe created? To some people this may tend to be a simple or silly question, but I assure you it is not. However, the average man would answer this question in this fashion: (1) the universe was created in the universe, at the same time not really understanding what the universe is even with his knowledge of religion, theology, divinity, philosophy, or, most of all, science. He also may reply: In the sky or in the heaven and in outer space.

However, I would say that this is indeed a hard question to answer from its beginning, *due to the fact that the where of the universe was first and foremost in the making. Its time, per se, was not of our time because of our nonexistence at that time. As to its "where" we really don't know because we came much later into it. Who is to say that it was always where it is now. Where is it now?* For now, to this day, science tells us that there could be no real center of the universe because of its form. *So if we can't determine its center, it would be even harder for us to determine its "where."* The question is both a physical and metaphysical one. So I would just simply say that the "where" of the universe is inside the vast spinning top of time. Why was the universe created? I don't know, except for the religious and philosophical statement that it was for God's own glory.

Who Created the Universe?

This question is in relation to the question Why was the Universe created? However, when I mentioned God, I am much like Einstein in his statement that I believe in the good of Spinoza, who reveals himself in a harmony of all creatures and not in a God who busies himself with the fate and action of man, a God who is not ANTHROPOMORPHIC, *because I, Faulkenstein, believes, in a sense, that God is an IDEA. A very real and big*

51

idea. Real and big as to the question yet to be answered, so for those who are still interested, they must keep looking.

How the Spinning Top Came to Be

To answer this is to ask the question, What spins the Spinning Top? I am trying to answer it all. *I have taken it upon myself to give this vast spinning top that we're in a name,* and in doing so the name itself would, in some way or another, explain these questions. The top that we're in, *as I have stated before, has a diameter of 200 decillion miles, with the velocity of 372,000 to 558,000 miles per second, consisting of everything known and unknown to us inside it,* at the same time with nothing existing outside of it. With this in mind, I have named this top, believable or unbelievable, that it may *be the META-PSEUDO-MICRO-MACROCOSMOS, meaning beyond the deceptive small microcosmos and solar system to the larger one, macro because our little microcosmos and solar system, large as it may seem to us, still has a much larger one beyond it. A macrocosmos unknown to us, yet to be explored.* Our universe, large as it may appear to us, is just a speck of micro (as vast and appears) to be as Einstein said 200 Sextillion miles. *Though Einstein may be right, Faulkenstein states that the spinning top has the diameter of 200 decillion miles, with our universe a speck inside it.* This would be the macrocosmos, though at the same time, our universe is inside the macro, and what motivates all of this? How did it come into being? To answer these questions, still I would have to say *TIME, time with its own personal self as the factor, and the main factor. Time has no form as we know it or physical or material elements, but it does, however, have a velocity.* So, therefore, *beginning and ending can not and should not apply to it; nor does life and death per se apply to time,* for the two are a part of time and nothing more. The same holds true for all things, material, natural, and physical. So time itself is the main factor, *and time needs none of these things to exist or prove its existence,* although all of these things came into being in TIME, and thus it marks their point.

There are three things that came into being without the help of man and long before man's time. *They are sound, light, and time*, though man uses them today for his own gain, and nature has given them to the lower kingdom of creatures for their own use and survival.

Sound

Sound itself has a velocity like light, but not as fast, and at the same time varies. *Sound in a substance has seven velocities as follows*: (1) air, 1,126 ft./sec.; (2) hydrogen, 4,315 ft./sec.; (3) carbon dioxide, 877 ft./sec.; (4) water, 4,820 ft./sec.; (5) iron or steel, 16,800 ft./sec.; (6) brass, 11,500 ft./sec.; and (7) granite, 12,960 ft./sec. *Now with this we can see how sound travels at different rates but still within some time period.*

Light

Light, too, we use for our own purpose, and science has given us much understanding concerning it. What science and Dr. Einstein, above all, has shown us is that in the theory of $E = mc^2$, light does not travel in a straight line, but curved somewhat because of our universe. *Also, light, like sound, has a velocity of 186,000 per second, the fastest motion known to us, and to ask the question what makes light travel?* is to ask the same question, What makes time travel or what spins the spinning top? Now we know what makes sound travel, but the same law of sound doesn't apply to light and the time top. However, we could say that rays of light, with its motions, energy, etc., motivates light. This may be true, but still the velocity among many scientists today as to how and not how fast is still in some cases argumentative. But since we and the world of science accept the velocity of light along with Einstein's theory of $E = mc^2$, we, therefore, except light's velocity as 186,000 miles per second.

Time

Time, per se, has already been explained; the only thing is that *we haven't noticed that time, too, has a velocity like light, with its velocity of 186,000 miles per second and sound with its different velocities.* So with this in mind, I am lead to believe that time, too, has a velocity. *Also, we must see, that it does not stand still.* It is a matter of measurement of all and everything, yet all and everything measure it. As the theory of $E = mc^2$ plus the theory of $M = T = CG \div$ sec., shows it to be a continuum meaning, never stopping but going on and on. In the laws of physics, sound and light are vital to man and the lower creatures; so is time. *Sound and light came into being in time; also time engulfs the two, and they can not be without time, plus time gives them a velocity, though different. Then, it's only natural and logical to see* that time doesn't stand still and these two high velocities, arriving out of time, are still a part of it. Time being the main factor, must have a velocity, and since light is the fastest of speed, as we know it according to Einstein, *then the theory of $M = T = CG \div$ sec., goes on to show us that not light but TIME is our fastest moving thing. Sound and light are a part of it. Since light is the fastest thing known to us, it is only natural and logical to see that time must be two to three times faster, 372,000-558,000 miles per second, going on and on but and the same time around and around.* As we have nothing made by us to factually measure the speed of light, so the same holds true for the speed of time. The only real way for us to do this is to make an object travel faster than the speed of light and then measure; to step outside the top and observe but this is impossible. *To make an object to measure the velocity of light is a great and high possibility, but to step outside time in order to measure its velocity is absolutely impossible.* So what is happening is that we moving with it, around and around, but not detecting it because our minds and bodies have over thousands of years been accustomed to it. It is only when we take it upon ourselves to spin our body around and around that we feel faint or dizzy. This is due to the fact that we are mixing time motion with our made motion; our bodies feel a chain reaction resulting in dizziness and faintness.

So, with this in mind, Faulkenstein's theory shows us that time is the fastest motion, with light second to it and sound shortly following. Also, we have many theories on the velocity of sound. We have other theories, as well as Dr. Einstein's of $E = mc^2$, on the velocity of light. Now, out of time, has come Faulkenstein's theory of $M = T = CG \div$ sec., giving us the velocity of time. We could say that the theory of $M = T = CG \div$ sec. is only imaginative and speculative; isn't this what most theories are until someone comes up with a better or more logical one? So though we cannot measure time's velocity with anything known to us, we may have, as I have stated before, even though time has a velocity. *So the theory of $M = T = CG \div$ Sec. is all METAPHYSICOTHEOLOGOCOSMOLOG-INGOLOGY. A metaphysicotheologocosmologingologist is a person or scientist who is learned or read in the fields of metaphysicotheologocosmologingology,* meaning the use of physics, plus metaphysics, theology, and cosmology, to explain the great topics, answers, and ideas of man, space time, mass energy, matter, substance, universe, God, and the like. So when a person or scientist uses physics, metaphysics, theology, and cosmology, all in one, then he is a metaphysicotheologocosmologingologist, and the knowledge of the same is like unto it, metaphysicotheologocosmologingology, such as $M = T = CG \div$ sec., and M. E. C. = G, and T = M. E. C. = G plus $T + A. E. = N.$

9

Newton's, Einstein's, and Faulkenstein's Universe

When one ring dies out, the pressure from the force inside the top will produce another—*Faulkenstein's fourth dimensional universe!* We must consider first of all that our big and vast universe, with the cosmos, solar system, and planets, stars, moons, and suns, is inside a much bigger and vaster spinning top that I call time.

Newton considered the nature of our universe on the basis of his laws of gravitation. He concluded that it consisted of all the stars and galaxies concentrated together at the center of the universe with no matter or other material existing in all the rest of the vast void beyond. He also concluded that our universe was like a finite island in an infinite ocean of space. *On the basis of the above, we would say that according to Newton, the universe was finite and unbounded.*

There were many who did not accept the Newtonian conception of the universe on philosophical grounds alone since it would mean that the light and energy continuously radiated by the stars would go off into the vast spaces beyond the stars, never to return. It seemed inconceivable that the universe would gradually dissipate its energy in this manner and eventually die out. It was also intellectually unsatisfying to have such a vast space beyond the stars without knowing what it was made up of or what was behind it.

On the basis of the general theory of relativity, Einstein was able to show that such a universe as depicted by Newton was unlikely, if not impossible, for mathematical reasons. In particular, he showed that in such a universe the average density of matter throughout the entire universe would have to be zero. The Laws of Newton were predicated on the fact that light traveled in a straight line. The general theory showed, however, that light rays are deflected by gravitational masses. *On the basis of the results of the general theory and his reasoning, Einstein originally concluded that our universe is finite and unbounded.*

Our universe is analogous to the surface of a sphere in two dimensions, which is finite and unbounded. If we travel in a straight line on the surface of a sphere (the earth, say), we will eventually come back to the starting point *without having consciously turned around anywhere during the journey. A straight line on the earth is one that follows the earth's surface. We know that the earth's surface is round, but we cannot detect this easily with the eye since the curvature is so slight.*

Out in space, a straight line is determined by the path a light beam takes. When it travels far away from gravitational masses, it is not influenced by them; but in their vicinity, the light is curved or bent toward the masses. For this reason, space itself is said to be curved; hence, the origin of such terms as space curvature or the curvature of space. *Space should not be imagined to be curved in the ordinary sense of the word* but only in that it contains gravitational masses (stars and other solar systems that may exist) that cause light rays to be deflected in their vicinity.

The property of gravitational masses to deflect light rays explains why our universe is unbounded. For although light rays travel in straight lines in the vast reaches of space between the stars, they will be deflected when passing near the stars. And if light rays suffer enough successive deflections, they can be caused to turn completely around and face in the opposite direction, in the same way the traveler does when he is halfway around the earth. And, like the earth voyager who returns to his starting point by continually traveling in a straight line on the earth's surface, *a space travler in our universe would also find himself back on earth if he travels what appears to him to be a straight line in space. He would no more know that he was traveling a gigantic circle in space than the earth voyager is conscious of traveling in a circle on the earth.* In general, a straight line in space, then, is the path a light beam takes, which may be straight or curved or a combination of both. In order to avoid confusion with what we ordinarily think *of as a straight line, we will refer to the lines in which light travels as space lines rather than straight lines in space.*

So if the Einstein conception of the universe is correct, a "space train" that leaves the earth and continually travels in a space line will always end up again at the earth regardless of what the original direction is away from the earth. And again, like the earth voyager, no barrier of any kind will be met during such a trip around our universe; *hence, our universe is unbounded.*

Our universe is finite because if you continually travel in a space line and end up at the starting point again a certain time later, only a finite amount of space would be passed through. And, again, like the surface of the sphere, this amount of space should be measurable.

The physical picture of our universe is that of a vast ocean of space with galaxies of stars (plus whatever other celestial material there might be) embedded in it in a more or less uniform distribution, like raisins in a loaf of raisin bread. (Some refer to the gravitational masses as "pimples in space," "kinks in space," or "ripples on the space surface.") *Moreover, there is no outside edge of the universe, for we have seen that continual travel in a space line brings you back to the starting point. Our universe closes on itself.*

The earth is shown at the center of the universe. (It must not be concluded from this that the earth is actually at the center of the universe since there is no such thing as a center of our universe any more than a center exists on a two-dimensional spherical surface.) If you travel outward from the central earth on one of the space lines, you will keep getting farther and farther away from the earth. On the two-dimensional spherical surface, this corresponds to getting farther and farther away from your starting point as you travel in a straight line on the earth's surface. At a certain distance, represented by the large circle, the space train will be at the maximum distance from the earth in the same way that the earth traveler is at a maximum distance from his starting point when he has reached a point on the earth diametrically opposite his starting point.

As the space train keeps on traveling along the space line, he will now find himself approaching the earth again. This is shown by the portions of the lines outside the circle converging toward the other earths. These earths really represent our earth at the center of a diagram, but to the space traveler who doesn't understand the nature of our universe, they will look like duplicates of our earth until he "gets down to earth" and finds that it is really the same earth he took off from. In the two-dimensional analogy, the earth traveler, too, eventually sees his starting point in front of him when he knows he left it behind him. If he did not understand the nature of his world, he, too, would think he was seeing a duplicate of his starting place.

Since there exists a maximum possible distance from the earth, we can look upon this distance as being the radius of the universe. This is again analogous to the spherical surface: for every point on it, there is another point diametrically opposite. The distance between the two points will, of course, depend on the radius of the sphere—the larger the radius, the greater the distance between the two points. For a sphere the size of the earth, for example, the point that is at the maximum distance from the North Pole is the South Pole.

Einstein was able to derive an expression for the radius of the universe; he found that it depended on the average density of matter in the universe. (Mathematically speaking, he found that the radius varies inversely as the square root of the density.) *Using the best "guestimate" for the average density of matter in space, the present conclusion is that the radius of the universe is about 200,000,000,000,000,000,000,000 miles.*

We can conclude that according to the general theory of

relativity, the universe was considered to be finite and unbounded. Whether it is or not may never actually be determined experimentally. However, it is amusing to predict what may take place many years from now.

Although Einstein's model of the universe was an intriguing one and was based on a rather firm mathematical foundation, an important development occurred in 1929 that completely invalidated it. For it was during that year that the American astronomer, Edwin P. Hubble, announced that on the basis of experimental evidence (the so-called "red shifts"), *it appeared as if all the other galaxies were rapidly running away from us. The interpretation of this is that our universe is in a state of very rapid expansion.*

This development nullifies *the original Einstein model of the universe* as elucidated in the preceding section because it was based on our universe *being static,* that is, *not expanding.*

Now Faulkenstein's universe on a fourth-dimensional plane. I have already mentioned how our universe with cosmos, solar system, etc., are all within a Celestial Globe. Now, with this in mind, along with Newton and Einstein's universe, I will try to show Newton's and Einstein's universe to be, to some degree, null and void.

First, with Newton's universe, in which he considered the stars and galaxies concentrated together at the center of the universe, with no matter or other material existing in all the rest of the vast void beyond, has been disproved by Einstein and other scientists in agreement with Einstein.

Second, Einstein stated that our universe does consist of other possible solar systems in the vast and void beyond. *He states that our universe, like Newton's is finite and unbounded.* He went further than Newton when he declared that our universe was not only finite and unbounded *and that there is no such thing as the center of the universe but that it has the radius of two hundred sextillion miles* (200,000,000,000,000,000,000,000) and at the same time is static, not expanding.

Now Faulkenstein, in relation to both Einstein and Newton, sees the universe or imagines it to be in a four-dimensional way:

1. Finite due to the fact that it is inside a big and vast spinning top that *has a diameter of two hundred decillion miles or more;*
2. Infinite due to the fact that Einstein states that it is curved or a curvature, for his special theory of relativity of lights has proved it;
3. Unbounded because of its curved form;
4. Bounded *because its radius of two hundred sextillion is still inside the invisible shell of two hundred-decillion-mile spinning top, at the velocity of 372,000-588,000 miles, per second and therefore sealed in.*

But, at the same time, unlike Einstein, *I believe it to be expanding but at the same time static;* expanding, as others have imagined, because the top, while spinning, inside our universe moves our stars up toward its top, which makes the stars, as others believe, move away from us. But, at the same time, they will not remain at the top because, as I said before, when an object is spinning fast, it will sooner or later be thrown out of these rings. When this happens, the form from these stars, as they get closer to our earth ring—we call these shooting stars—will, as they are traveling, burn up, die out, or in other ways hit the earth and crash as comets or meteorites sometimes do.

I believe it to be static because as long as our universe is bounded by the inside shell of the 372,000-558,000 miles per second spinning top with the diameter of two hundred decillion miles or more, *it can not expand but only appear to be doing so.* Also, this vast and big spinning top with its diameter, I believe to be two hundred decillion miles or more and with the velocity of 372,000-558,000 miles per second, I consider time, forever and ever spinning, on and on. The fourth dimension, though,. I say, has no form to it as form that we know but an unknown form known to us all as time, for time's sake.

However, as a religionist, God's universe, when we come right down to it, is still a big mystery to us all. Be it Newton's, Einstein's, or mine, it is still all a mystery. God's mystery—only he, as the first scientist and metaphysician, knows its real and hidden truth.

So there we have it, our universe. *It is finite* because it is limited by the top. Infinite, thus, because we cannot go outside the universe. *Unbounded* because it is curved *and at the same time bounded* because it is sealed within the top. The fourth dimension, time!

10

The Spinning-Top Theory

Science and scientists now accept the fact that the earth moves in its orbit around the sun with the velocity of *about nineteen miles per second.*

Scientists also believe that light will go completely around the earth in a seventh of a second, and it takes about eight minutes for sunlight to travel the 93,000,000 miles from the sun to the earth. Thus, in the morning when you awake and see the sun come up, it has been or actually risen eight minutes before. In this respect, no one on earth ever sees the sun come up. So since it takes eight minutes for the sunlight to travel from the sun to the earth, we can say that the sun is eight minutes away by light in the same way we say that Stamford is forty miles from New York City by rail. *The nearest star to us beyond the sun is Alpha-Centauri, which is about four light years away.* This means that it would take us four years to get there if we traveled by light. *One light year is 6,000,000,000,000 miles. Alpha-Centauri is about 24,000,000,000,000 miles away,* which is a long way for a next-door neighbor!

Einstein's theory of relativity applied to that of relative motion states that the behavior of *lights waves was not influenced in any way by the movement of the earth through space.* So the same thing should apply to the big spinning top of time, with the speed of light traveling through it. *For the speed of time is not in any way influenced by the speed of light, per se;* if so, then in measurement only, and since time is two to three times faster than the speed of light, 372,000 to 558,000 miles per second.

Please note that James A. Coleman, *Relativity for the Layman,* 1958, states that the reason the theory of relativity is in general looked upon as being incomprehensive is not because the results are difficult to understand but that they are difficult to believe. *The same opinion could be applied to the split-second theory of $T = M = CG \div sec.$*

The book *The Universe,* by David Bergamini, published by *Life* in 1962, states, starting on page 169, that in many ways the universe revealed by Hubble is the essence of simplicity. It is expanding a bubbleful of hot gas suddenly released in a vacuum. Each galaxy is like a molecule in the gas. As the cloud expands, *every molecule in it will double its distance from every other molecule in the same period of time.* After a second period of time twice as long as the first, the doubling will take place again— and so on ad infinitum. During this uniform expansion, a *theoretical external observer can always tell that the molecule at the center of the cloud is stationary. But an observer on the central molecule itself may not be able to tell that he is stationary.* The outrushing of nearby molecules around him appears exactly the same as if he were riding a moving molecule. *Only if he can see out to the edges of the cloud* and count the molecules in every direction can he make sure that he is at the center of the cloud.

This is the same thing as the spinning top that we're in, at its velocity of 372,000-558,000 miles per second. But being inside of it and at the same time moving along with it, we would not and do not notice this *unless we could step outside of the top and observe. Would we know or really see just how fast we're moving along with everything else in the top?*

Since modern astronomers can detect galaxies receding at nearly nine-tenths the enormous 186,000 miles per second speed of light, and since they have not yet found any outer edge to the universe, they are convinced that the cosmos is not so simple as a mere puff of uniformly expanding gas that has partly condensed into galaxies. This has already been explained in the theory of $M = T = CG \div$ sec., where it states that this part just mentioned is true due to the fact that the universe inside the top is spinning so fast that the results are as just mentioned.

For the universe to be understandable, the sample of it included with this cosmic horizon must be large enough to reveal the overall cosmos structure. And once again cosmologists have reason to be optimistic. The speed of light is a fundamental constant of nature. Within the context of any one fixed frame of measurement like the solar system, light has the ultimate velocity. In cyclotrons, atomic particles, accelerated to nearly the speed of light, resist further pushing as if they were growing more and more massive. They act as if, upon reaching the speed of light, they would become infinitely massive—"heavier" than all the galaxies put together. *In the universe, the speed of light does not limit the speed of galaxies in quite the same straightforward way. But it crops up in cosmologists' equations at critical moments—so much so that in almost every mathematical theory of the universe proposed up to now, the speed of light partly determines the overall cosmic structure.* For science tells us that this may be true up until now, but the theory of $M = T = CG \div$ sec. shows us that the speed of time, 372,000-558,000 miles per second, *should now determine the overall cosmic structure. Light is no longer the main factor, but the second, with time now being the first. Light is inside it and relative to it, while at the same time our universe, cosmos, earth, and the like are relative to it, and so on. But all this relativity is inside the main factor time,* the spinning top of 372,000-558,000 miles per second. What was just stated from the book *The Universe* in reference to the fact that in the universe the speed of light does not limit the speed of the galaxies in quite the same straightforward way *only brings out that the theory of $M = T = CG \div$ sec. shows us that we are moving as well as everything else known and unknown to us at a velocity two to three times the velocity of light.* We have no physical instrument made by us or known to us to travel at the velocity of light, only instruments to surpass that of the speed of sound. So because we have nothing to measure the velocity of light, *we give light first priority.* But now with the split-second theory, *we can see that we are moving much faster than light, and light is only an imaginative secondary factor when it comes to the main factor, time.* Only in man-made, man-motivated instruments do we praise and put light on a higher and more elevated plane. Time's velocity is the main factor with the velocity of light inside it, and the velocity of galaxies, missiles, jet planes, and the like still inside it, at the same time a part of it, though at the same time not always motivated by it.

So, when it comes to velocity, this is what we have: (1) $E = mc^2$, light, 186,000; (2) sound, 750 miles per hour; and (3) time, $M = T = CG \div$ sec., 372,000-558,000 miles per second, which engulfs the first two and the velocity of velocities known to us. *The reason why I mentioned sound, light, and time is because these are the only factors that are independent. We have no control over them originally, and we did not invent them.* They are independent, because they are of completely themselves. Two, no control originally because we did not invent them, though we use them all. And, third, we have only rediscovered them. We use and create different kinds of light, but still light's velocity we can not precede. Sound we precede in velocity, but still sound came into its being without us, man, though we make sound; we make it because it was and is. And time, a mystery to us up until $M = T = CG \div$ sec., but still to some extent a mystery. Time we can not create, only things that are a part of time or that came into being in time. Time we can not really control and will never outlive. Nothing but nothing can outlast time because as long as time has no life, as we know it, it will never have any death as we know it. All things in time will reach an end, rock, steel, iron, everything, but not time. Time has a velocity of 372,000-558,000 miles per second, in a diameter of 200 decillion miles, and with everything that is inside it, and outside it, there is nothing. While time is, it just keeps on velocifying on and on, independent of itself; it measures all things, while at the same time all things can't measure it. Man, with his small intelligence, does snatch a part of time and put his measurements to it for his own use but not always to his own good. The little part he snatches will outlast him in one way and leave him quickly in another. When it outlasts him, he dies, and when he outlasts it, he says, Wow, time sure has gone fast, or, Where did time go? Or, What have I done with all the time I had?

So, with this in mind, you can use $M = T = CG \div$ sec. to better understand just what you're in and how it affects you, all and everything. Yes, by the time I finish writing this, I would be, according to $M = T = CG \div$ sec., 7,476,800 years old, at the velocity of 558,000 miles per second, plus three years every second; 180 year every minute; 10,800 every hour; and 258,200 years every day.

By the way, how old are you?

11

Human Biological Change
and the Spinning Top

When it comes to our material bodies and human bodies aging
(1) 2 to 3 years every second and (2) 120 to 180 years every
minute, we should think in nowise this to be ironic. We have
many modern medical reports on the human body, and their
discoveries, and I intend to prove or show you how these medical
reports in one way or another coincides with $M = T = CG \div$
sec., concerning our age and human body functions and changes.
So to start with, let's consider what medical science states about
our body cells. (1) *The human body renews 3 billion cells every
minute;* (2) *it takes the average human body 10 billion cells to
read one page of anything;* (3) *there is a network of some 60,000
miles of tubing that carries blood to every part of the body;*
(4) its most impressive feature is the circular manner in which
it keeps the blood moving, always from the heart to the arteries,
toward the heart in the veins in spite of gravity and in spite of
millions of alternative routes. The pump of the heart gives the
flow its force, sending freshly oxygenated blood surging out the
aorta, the body's largest artery, and into subsidary arteries, even
to the top of the head. The arteries branch out into smaller
arterioles, *which, in turn, branch out into millions of microscopic
capillaries.* These capillaries eventually unite to form venules,

which unite into veins, thin-walled vessels with interior valves that prevent the blood from slipping backward. Thus, the spent blood streams back to the heart. A side trip to the lungs via a pulmonary network refreshes it with oxygen, and it returns to the heart to start anew. *The entire cycle takes less than a minute.* (5) *A mature body contains more than 600 muscles and 206 bones,* not counting the tiny sesamoid bones—like sesame seeds—embedded in the tendons of the thumb, big toe and other pressure points. For the bones, in fact, this represents a comedown; newborn babies may not have more than 300. By adulthood many of these bones have fused. Not infrequently, however, fusion fails. An otherwise average person may find himself with an extra bone in the arch of the foot, *and one in every twenty people has an extra rib. This appendage appears three times as often in men as in women—possibly a form of compensation for the rib Adam yielded to Eve.* Except for these minor anomalies, the arrangement of the bones is as precise, orderly, and purposeful as the parent skeletal system itself, and their distribution from top to bottom is a strikingly equitable one. *The skull at the apex of the bony structure has twenty-nine bones. The spine, to which are attached the shoulder girdle, rib cage, and hip girdle, has twenty-six vertebrae. The ribs number twenty-four.* (6) The teeming traffic of the busiest metropolis presents a study in sheer inertia when compared to the ceaseless activity within our own bodies. Day and night, loading and unloading goes on at every one of the body's trillions of cells. Food and oxygen are taken on; waste products are taken off. The process slows somewhat during sleep, but it never halts. A stoppage would, indeed, signal death.

Like a great city, the body needs a transport system to carry its vital cargoes to and fro. This network—the circulatory, or cardiovascular, system—has its freeways, underpasses, cloverleafs, subsidiary roads, quiet streets, and back alleys. In the nomenclature of the body, the lines of supply bear the labels of artery, arteriole, capillary, venule, and vein. *The total distance they cover, within the confines of the body, is estimated at 60,000 miles.*

The major means of transport within this vast complex is blood. Its flow is controlled by the heart. Under impetus of the heart's pumping action, the blood, with its freight, makes continuous round trips, without pause, in and out of the heart, through the rest of the body, and back into the heart, to be sent out again. The heart pumps so steadily and powerfully that in a *single day it pushes ten pints of blood in the average adult body through more than 1,000 complete circuits, thus actually pumping 5,000 to 6,000 quarts of blood a day in all. (7) Our brain weighs no more than three pounds, and there are 250,000 to 2.5 million cells to the human body or more.* Man with these great activities of the human body and its constant changes in cells, *by the number of 3 billion every minute.* This could be brought about due to the fact that we are in the time celestial globe with the velocity of 372,000-558,000 miles per second, and aging 2-3 years every second, 120-180 years every minute, 7,200-10,800 years every hour, and 172,800-259,200 years old every day. *So as we age, each second, minute, hour, and day, so are we accumulating 3 billion cells each minute, 180 billion per hour, and 4,320 trillion each day. As we renew our body cells by the billion, so are we at the same time aging in the thousands and millions with this kind of activity and energy.* Medical science shows us that this is a form of regeneration, and at the same time, $M = T = CG \div$ sec. shows us that we are at the same time regenerating and degenerating until our body over a period of time cannot produce the necessary cells or sustain itself against time with the producing rate of age, until degeneration comes about with more degeneration, until finally death—*death not at the age of forty-five, fifty, sixty-five or more but death at the age of of 16 billion 348 million, as the theory of $M = T = CG \div$ sec. shows us.* To discover this equation is done, go back in the theory where it first states that we are in a time celestial globe, moving at the velocity of two to three times the velocity of light—light, 186,000 miles per second. Time, which is in the time spinning top or globe, has a velocity of 372,000-558,000 miles per second.

70

How to calculate your age according to $M = T = CG \div$ sec.

Example: eighteen years old today, twice the velocity of light.

1 second; 2 years old
60 seconds; 120 years
1 hour = 7,200 years
1 day = 172,800 years
172,800 x 30 (for one month) times that answer by twelve for one year

Then multiply that answer by 18, as your age is now, and you will come up with the total. Plus the on coming extra seconds.

One can follow the same procedure with the velocity three times that of light.

The last two answers equalling 172,800 years, or one day = 259.200 is multiplied by thirty for one month by twelve months would give you your age for one year as we know it. Multiplying by the person's present age would give the total answer.

12

M. E. C. = G.

In reference Faulkenstein's Theory of $M = T = CG \div$ sec. concerning how the spinning top or time capsule globe came into being, what spins it? Wayne Trader, a friend of mine, and I came up with a second theory to these questions in which I named the M. E. C. = G, meaning the massive energic cell. This cell, to begin with, controls, motivates, and activates all and everything inside the top. This massive energic cell, I believe: (1) has always been in existence; (2) engulfs each and everything but at the same time produces and reproduces and creates everything known and unknown to us; (3) *can shape itself by intelligence, unknown to us as intelligence, to any form or fashion that it chooses known and unknown to us;* (4) that all and everything came from it; (5) that the spinning top, as vast as it is, with its 200 decillion miles, is a very small part of M. E. C. = G; (6) that M. E. C. = G has no time formula as we know time, and, therefore, to us, it has no beginning or ending; and (7) that philosophically or in a philosophical, scientific way, M. E. C. = G is God. *Therefore, all energy small and large, known and unknown to us, is God = M. E. C.*

When I stated earlier, in the theory of $M = T = CG \div$ sec., that everything known and unknown to us is inside the top or spinning celestial globe, this in no way applied to God. As the theory of M. E. C. = G shows, the spinning top with its vastness of 200 decillion miles accelerating at the velocity of 372,000-558,000 miles per second, produces and reproduces each and everything known and unknown to us inside it, even if by our own minds and hands within seconds and split seconds, but at the same time unnoticable to us and, I might add, unbelievable. *The M. E. C. = G is a part of the spinning top but at the same time outside of it and remaining a massive energic cell,* still in many ways unknown to us. Why? Because (1) our minds are so small and too limited to comprehend M. E. C. = G in its fullness. (2) *We factually don't know God, but only the word God and what it's supposed to religiously imply. So all we do is believe, hope and pray and have faith in Him or It.* (3) If God didn't create man, man out of his own weakness and insecurity would have sooner or later created God because of his constant dependence to need someone or something to lean on and, at the same time, *something extrasuper to believe in.* (4) With Number 2 and Number 3, in mind, we are confronted by the age old questions, *Did God as the Bible states create man, or did man out of his own imagination create God?*

Well, as I have already stated, like Spinoza, Einstein, Wayne Trader, and many other scientists, I believe in the God who reveals himself in a harmony of all creatures and living things and not just the God who busies himself with the fate and action of men. The theory of M = T = CG ÷ sec., shows us the real, true, and better understanding and character of M. E. C. = G, such as: (1) when there is birth in all living creatures, high or low; (2) growth in plants and agriculture; (3) the constant rising and setting of the sun; (4) the light and wonders of the moon and other planets, with their moons, suns, stars, and mystery, still unknown to us about our vast and expanding universe, and much, much more. *I have come to believe, among other things that God is an idea. A very real and big idea, as big as the questions yet to be answered factually.* So for those who are still interested, they must keep looking. And now we come back to the meaning of idea! As we know, ideas are (1) formed in the minds of man and only man. (2) *In this mind of man is the home of imagination.* (3) My imagination has lead me to believe and visualize God and his works in the theory of $M = T = CG \div$ sec. From out of $M = T = CG \div$ sec. has come the theory or idea of $M. E. C. = G$, who is spinning and activating it all as well as us all.

Now, with all of this in mind, can you see the deep insight of all this? $M = T = CG \div sec.$, *motivated and activated as well as created by M. E. C. = G.* However, I have not forgotten that religions and the Bible teach that God is a spirit. Well, this may be, and I will not argue the questions because this is not the purpose of the two theories. *My theories are to give the reader and the world a better understanding of God,* man, universe, time, space, matter, energy, etc., for today and possibly tomorrow, if there is such a thing. *I am not only concerned with the questions as to whether or not God created all things, but I'm concerned with how He did it,* not with the question Is God really a spirit? All powerful? All knowing? All big? *By way of my theory, could a spirit be a cell, all powerful, every kind of energy known or unknown to us,* all knowing, a higher and much bigger intelligence that we could possibly never get to know or understand. Therefore, God today remains a mystery to us. *The vastness of this cell equals God, the M. E. C. = G* (the massive energic cell = God). *With this in mind, we should see God in a more clear scientific and religious light.* M.E.C. is constantly active and regenerating, so we as part of it, or in its image of some form are constantly active as medical science shows us. Our bodies renew 3 billion cells per minute, while I contribute this active energic change in us by our being in the spinning top, moving at the velocity of 372,000-588,000 miles per second. Not only are we renewing our body cells but at the same time aging 120 to 180 years every minute.

My research on the subject of time, mass, matter, energy, and the universe has lead me to a book of some fourteen years in print, 1958, by Harlow Shapley, entitled, of Stars and Men. The author of this book came very close to expressing my theories of $M = T = CG \div$ sec. and M. E. C. = G. The reason I have at length chosen this book for some of its selections is that it gives

74

us a better scientific understanding of the chemical makeup of all living things as well as other matters, objects, and the like. So now let's see what Mr. Shapley has to say!

The discovery of the vastness of the universe that is open for life, the growing conviction that appeal to the supernatural is unnecessary for the beginning and evolution of living organisms, and the fresh ideas now evolving from other living human enterprise should be sufficient justification for a reconsideration, from time to time, of man's situation and function in the cosmos.

In view of the foregoing argument, we accept the appropriateness of a further inquiry into the human response to the facts and the viewpoint revealed by current scientific research. As an initial step in the approach to the central questions about the universe—that is, to the question "What, How and Why"—we shall consider briefly the formal subject of cosmography. Among other intentions, cosmography is a research attempt to solve the most intriguing placement problems in the world—the question of the location of man in the universe of space, atoms, and light. Actually the end product of our efforts may be only an approach to knowledge of man's orientation in a complex cosmos, not an arrival. Questions without answers will be a recurrent by product.

Again we define cosmography loosely as the field of study that has the same relation to the cosmos as geography has to the earth*. Such a definition requires a prior definition of the cosmos, and that is difficult. We shall see later that cosmos means something more than the physical universe. Nevertheless, even though not sharply defined. Cosmography remains a science—a science with decorations. If at times it sounds a bit like scientific philosophy, or even

---

**Cosmogony and Cosmology are related words frequently confused with cosmography,* and apparently ambiguous even to the lexicographer; the first, however, generally implies pretensions to knowledge of first origins; the second is commonly defined as a branch of metaphysics.

like a phase of religious teaching, so much the better. *It will be no loss for religion and philosophy if they are infiltrated with atoms, stars, and the groping of protozoa.*

For the time being at least we shall try to keep our explorations of cosmic content and activity on the descriptive level. Although cosmography as here presented is an elementary science, it carries a considerable intellectual voltage, enough to charge to full capacity the more sophisticated inquirer, enough to shock the casual and uninitiated.

Whatever else of significance we may later fabricate for life, it early becomes evident that the study of living things can contribute richly to Cosmography. An outstanding example is the direct association of chlorophyll with the age and structure of the sun and stars. This strange association ties the complicated chemical operation of photosynthesis with the internal anatomy of stellar bodies. The primitive plants of the Archeozoic Era, the green algae, were operating the photosynthetic apparatus more than a thousand million years ago; the complex leaves of the late Carboniferous plants also testify to a sun power that has been essentially constant from then to now. *The Paleozoic leaves testify that three hundred million years ago the solar radiation was little if any different from that we know now. The unhurried evolution of stars (at least of one star, the sun) is thus revealed by the Carboniferous ferns. A slow evolution is indicated, but how is it managed? What can be the source of the solar power that radiated energy into space at the rate of more than four million tons a second and yet does not exhaust itself over the millions of years?*

The full story is too long for this essay. We simply report that to energize the ancient alegae and the tree ferns of the Paleozoic, as well as modern plants, and activate the animals (including us) that are parasites on the plants, the sun transmutes hydrogen into helium and radiation, thus providing abundant energy. Fortunately for us, the radiant energy is issued by a self-regulating power plant.

The collaboration of the various sciences here is nicely

shown. Geochemistry, radiology, stratigraphy, atomic physics, and astronomy combine in the clear indication that matter can dissolve into radiation. The fossil plants (and animals), we learn by the way of paleontology, indicate the consistancy of the sun's heat and thus, by way of mathematical physics and astrophysics, reveal much about the internal structure of stars.

There are many other tie-ups with biology in the study of the inanimate universe. In the running of ants we can measure an energy flow that is as closely controlled by temperature as the outpouring of energy from distant stars. To study adequately the early climates of this planet we must bring together the methods and facts from a dozen scientific fields, some of them biological, some physical. When we see that many rules of nature are the same for biological cells and for chemical molecules, and when, as later elaborated, we accept the very impressive probability of millions of planets with highly developed organisms, we must conclude that the world of life should be admitted as a part of the cosmographic program.

Cosmography, when ideally described and studied involves an extensive and complicated content. It is too comprehensive to be handled thoroughly in brief compass. It appears to be manageable, however, if used chiefly as an instrument in human orientation. In what follows in this chapter we shall report on an attempt to survey sketchily the material universe, with principal emphasis on the basis entities, and on the extent to which the exploration of them and with them appears to pinpoint terrestrial man in the over-all scheme.

Our sense organs are definitely limited in number and power, and our experience in thinking about the cosmos has extended through only a few millennia—scarcely more than a dozen of the revolutions of the outermost planet Pluto. Too much should not be expected of us. We are tyros in the project of cosmic interpretation. Our accomplishments appear to be rather substantial when we look into the past, but have we not unrolled as yet only a fringe of one page of the total Cosmic Writ?

From where we now stand in knowledge of the world it appears that the basic entities of the material universe are the simple-sounding "qualities" or entities of space, time, and energy. Of the four, we note that matter and energy are two forms of the same thing, tied together with the most popular equation of our times (after $2 + 2 = 4$), namely, $E = mc^2$. That equations says that to transform mass, M, into energy, E, or energy into mass in a quantitative fashion we simply apply the square of that most fundamental of natural units, c, the velocity of light. By way of the relativity theory, also space and time are now commonly united as space-time.

A few thousand years ago the elementary alphabets began to appear. They came in the form of ABC's and the 1, 2, 3's. The letters could be formed into words to represent ideas, and in the various isolated cultures the words became standardized. They were formed into phrases, the phrases into sentences, and in some of the higher cultures the sentences were assembled into chapters, books and libraries.

The number was basic in primitive economics, and, with the ABC's eventually produced the business operations of the modern. The numbers led to our system of weights and measures. Without these alphabets—the letters and the numbers—we would culturally be little advanced beyond the birds, bees, and apes.

Two other elementary alphabets have long existed. One is connected with the entity Time and the other with the entity Space. They are, respectively, the calendars of days, weeks, months, and years, and the maps that record space measures on the face of the earth, that is, record the terrestrial latitudes and longitudes which permit the delimitation of fields, cities, and states.

These elementary alphabets no longer suffice, either in the study of Cosmography, or in any general effort of trying to understand a world that has become enormously rich in information content. They met our needs up to a century or so ago. With the growth in amount of information, however, it has become necessary to supplement the elementary alphabets, and introduce logical classifications. Well-organized, small tabular categories have been set up to facilitate the acquiring of knowledge about stars, atoms, plant varieties, rock series, and the like. These tables, in a way, are minor and specialized alphabets.

To assist further in our study, it is now proposed to construct a major comprehensive alphabet for each of the four entities: time, matter, space and energy. Through the use of these tabulations we shall simplify the natural complexities arising from so much specific information. *Fortunately, two of these basic tabulations are already at hand, perfected and in professional use. They are the periodic table of the elements for matter, and the geological age scale for time. The former concerns matter in its elemental forms; the latter, time in large chunks.* We shall begin, however, with a new table that is specially designed to attain our orientation in space—but first a digression. *In order to study these tables the reader is subjected to purchase the book entitled: Of Stars and Men, by Harlow Shapley.*

As scientists and dreamers we are curious about our position in the plan of the universe. Curious also about the "planning," and sometimes included to talk about the planner. *It is a fascination enterprise.* We can have a stimulating and in the end a satisfying experience in contemplating cosmographic facts and speculating on human fate and fancy.

The orientation of man is of course an absorbing subject, in part because he is an awkward and somewhat vain animal, but more because he is, whether he knows it or not, aimed at the stars. However ruthless he may have been in his jungle childhood and during his unsocial past, he is not instinctively ethical, not so much because virtue may please his tribal gods but because it is good economic and social policy. He is bent also on comprehension. Moreover, to make an anticipatory statement, man knows that he is participating, at a high and complex level, in a great evolutionary drive; he is going along, for the most part cheerfully, with such companions as the vibrating atoms, the radiating stars, the condensing nebulae, the groping protozoa, and the perennial forests with their aspiring birds and butterflies.

As cosmographers we enjoy the decipherment of some of the rules of the cosmic game. We salute the biological winners when we recognize them, such as the fish and the club mosses which can trace their ancestry of unchanged forms through many geological periods; and we can try to understand the losers, such as the trilobites of the early Paleozoic period, the dinosaurs of a hundred million years ago, and Neanderthal Man.

We also occasionally venture to the borders of science to seek deep answers and to discuss our hopes of contributing to future ages something more than our fragmented skulls in the fossiliferous rock. Naturally we are proud of the varied beauty of human thought and action, proud of our poetry and song. We are actors in a great cosmic play where the performers include the atoms, the galaxies, and the eternal intangibles.

The prophets of ancient Israel gloried at times in the magnificence of the universe, which of course, in their time, was centered on man. Those days, however, were scientifically very early and chronologically perhaps more than a third of the way back to the beginning of human cultures. What the inquiring mind has since uncovered would have been incredible if revealed to the ancient prophets. Their vision, was, we now see, myopic. Our vision is doubtless also deficient, but at least we recognize that we are taking part in a play far grander than foretold in ancient time. The advance notice of two to three millennia ago greatly underestimated the cosmic drama. Reverence then had to be supported with imaginings and superstition. But the accepted facts of now far transcend the fictions of not so long ago.

So it seems, at any rate, to those who look downward into atoms and the biological call and upward to the stars. To be reverent, we now have no need of superstitional aid.

In our cosmic inquiries we may appear boastful with regard to the inadequacies of the ancient philosophies, but we should suffer a healthy pride-shrinking experience in foreseeing that a century hence we, too, may be considered to have been primitives in knowledge and thought. Indeed, two of the present goals of the exploration among galaxies and atoms, are the same goals that should prevail in other fields of science, namely, to strengthen the evidence on which we can construct our current understanding and to contribute through research as rapidly as possible to the obsolescence of our presently cherished hypotheses. We hope for greater knowledge and sounder ideas in the future. *Deeper thoughts will surely come, wider spread of the senses, fuller appreciation of the functioning of the human brain,* higher ambitions for men participating in the greatest operation of nature— an operation of cosmic dimensions that might simply be called Growth.

In the microcosmic inanimate world the organizational tendencies are governed by electrostatic and similar forces. The fundamental particles (electrons, neutrons, etc.) organize first into atoms, then the atoms into molecules, and molecular systems, and on to larger and more complex organizations in the crystals and colloids.

With each higher organizations, as with human society, the elemental freedoms are increasing cramped. The wild liberties of an atom in the vacuum of intergalactic space have been largely lost to the molecules of oxygen and nitrogen in a closed room, where the air is earthbounded by gravitation and the incessant collisions prevent any one molecule from getting anywhere. And the atomic units of solid metals of my pencil are so much further cramped, confined and controlled that I do have a pencil. It is composed of agitated electrons protons, and neutrons that cannot freely escape into the interplanetary spaces. Always for the advantage of organization, the price is the loss of elemental freedom. A civilization, for example, costs much in loss of individual liberties, since excesses in freedom would lead to deficits in security and social advantage. The freely roaming and unpoliced dinosaurs, I like to remember, had no plumbing.

As we proceed to greater and more massive organizations, we begin to leave the microcosmos at the colloidal level. We enter the macrocosmic world where gravitation appears as the effective control. In the sidereal realm, we find dust particles assembling into proto-stars, with gas pressure and radiation opposing the dominating gravitation. Stars frequently appear in pairs and triples. Star cluster and clouds of stars are next in magnitudes of stellar organization, and these, with the scatter single and multiple stars, are congregated into the great cosmic units called galaxies. A continuous sequence, we find, from atoms to the Metagalaxy.

Geological Ages—A Higher Alphabet for Time

Looking again at our listing of material systems that extend from subelectrons to the space-time complex and beyond, we are impressed by the fact that motion prevails throughout the long series. Everything is moving. The movements are relative to various zeros or coordinates, or with respect to bodies of similar or different character. *The radiation quantum respects and energy transfer in space with the speed of light, and the electrons in the atom move at tremendous speeds, according to commonly accepted atomic models.* But such light velocities are not common. Some of the relative motions, like those of crystals fixed in rock, differ immeasurably from zero. Other slow motions are those of plants and animals on a planetary surface. Intermediate speeds include the velocity of a comet in passage around a star, and the recession of nearby galaxies, in an expanding universe.

Notwithstanding its universality, motion is hardly a fundamental or basic entity of the material universe. *It is a change of position, the speed of a change is measured as space (length) divided by time. The prevalence of motion everywhere emphasizes, therefore, that time is a basic factor in the career of material systems. Growth and decay are time linked. Organizations can fade away. Comets, for example, dissolve; open star clusters are slowly dismembered by gravitational shearing; molecules are forced by radiation to dissociates; organic bodies rot, and nations decay.* Also, organizations of all sort, physical and biological, have emerged in the course of time out of uncoordinated prestuff of various kinds. Most of them grow slowly in complexity and volume, some speedily by mutations.

The time element everywhere enters the panorama of the universe. We can aid our understanding of origins and growth, of decay and death by an alphabetization of time intervals, much as our space concepts are aided by the table of material systems.

For the full descriptions of operations in the material universe that involve temporal sequences, we need a very comprehensive calendar. *In fact, we need many kinds of clocks, and calendars, tuned to the many various needs. Those that now conveniently hang in the office and home are of no use in timing the laboratory's transmutation of hydrogen atoms into helium or the explosive release of the atomic energy that runs the stars.* Nor on the other hand are such calendars useful in considering the relatively slow evolution of beetles or the rotation of a galaxy. The intervals are too coarse for electrons, too fine for mountain building. *For the latter, however, a most impressive calendar is already at hand—the geological age table.*

One of the most fortunate breaks that has come to inquiring mankind, in addition to the provision of his relatively large cerebral cortex, is his having evolved on the surface of a planet that is extremely old. Probably the first life forms, and certainly the oldest rocks of the earth's crust, were already in existence in the very early days of our expanding universe. When the trilobites dominated the shallow seas, the galaxies were much closer together than in the present years. Many of our brightest stars, it is now believed, were born long after the great Mesozoic lizards disappeared. We can, if we will, use our geological calendar astronomically and speak of Pliocene stars and Cretaceous galaxies.

If our planet and its sentient life, including mankind, had been the product of a recent sidereal event, say 5,000 years ago, instead of the product of stellar violence that dates back 5,109,000 years we would have found it hard to discover the origin of stellar energy and to estimate the age of the stars. Our base line would have been too short. We are, indeed, fortunate to be established on a relatively steady and very ancient crust.

Since prehistoric times the rotation of the earth in the vacuum of surrounding space has been accepted as our best timekeeper. In pre-Copernican times nearly everyone misidentified the rotation as the daily trip of the sun around the fixed earth, but that presumption only transferred timekeeping to the sun and stars. The earth's rotation was and is measured against the distant stars, used as fixed reference points, and its period, the day, is known with astounding accuracy—to a millionth of a second. But that is not good enough for modern science. The earth's rotation is slightly disturbed by the variable distribution each year of polar snow and ice; and there are internal adjustments of the rock layers beneath the surface of the earth which can also effect its regularity. Moreover, the moon through its production of tides in the earth's air, water, and land, acts as a brake on the rotation; the same for the sun, but less effective because more distant.

The earth's incompetence as a keeper of the most highly accurate time has incited the development of ingenious timekeepers, such as those involving the very precise pendulum slave clocks, and the vibrations of crystals and of the atoms inside the modecules of ammonia. Other atomic timepieces are currently under development.

The pulsating and eclipsing variable stars are also celestial timekeepers but in practice of low accuracy; and likewise the circling satellites of Jupiter and Saturn. *The revolving of our sun around the center of the galaxy provides a time unit of some two hundred million terrestrial years, with an uncertainty, however, not in seconds or days or months, but in millions of years.* This big time union, the cosmic year, even though only roughly known, is of interest when we consider the transformation of galaxies from one type to another. It enters in predicting the time necessary to dissolve the Pleiades, and in speculating on the age of our Milky Way.

The most impressive and useful calendar for Cosmography, however, is that provided by the spontaneous and natural decay of uranium, thorium and other radioactive elements that are embedded in the rocks of the earth's crust. *Paradoxically, the micro-micro seconds of the radioactive atomic transformation are involved in the construction of the geological calendar for which the millennia are the time units.* We see the briefest to measure the longest.

As with the timing of a galactic rotation, the percentage accuracy for geological dating is not high. Nevertheless, this Calendar of the Eras is one of the prize threads of information that man has laborously unraveled.

Associated with the radioactive rocks, where the automatically decaying atoms of uranium grow fewer with time while the end products, helium and lead, grow more, we find the fossils of ancient life. We find bones, sometimes, and shells, leaf traces, seeds, and tracks in the ancient fossilized sands and mud. We properly assume that the age of the rocks, which radioactivity measures, is also the age of the fossils. From their own standpoint the animals and plants of past eras are very dead, but they are exceedingly alive in our reconstruction of the story and tempo of biological evolution. The distribution, nature and age of these fossils also assist in solving the puzzles of the origin of our planet and the secrets of its early days. Again we note that some of the fossil plants in the rocks testify eloquently to the long dependability of sunlight as we know it.

The geological time table, as it has now been worked out by investigators in geology, radiology, paleontology, geophysics, and geochemistry, provides a fairly good calendar back to the beginning of the Cambrian Era five hundred million years ago (Table II). It also roughly dates the much older igneous rocks that are associated with the most ancient dim records of simple algae and fungi. These records are scanty and not too sure, but they suggest an age of at least fifteen hundred million years for organisms that knew how to use sunlight for energy.

Although uranium, radium, thorium, helium and lead were the principal original elements involved in the construction of the radioactivity-based cosmic calendar, several other chemical elements are now used in the dating of fossils, rocks and human artifacts. Among them are *potassium* decaying into *calcium* and *argon, rubidium into strontium,* and the relative abundance of *isotopes of oxygen and of carbon.* Probably additional elements will become useful as techniques improve. The timetable has increasingly validity.

The geological eras and periods, with the times of their beginnings, and a reference to their biology, are given in Table II without subdivision and without further comments at this point on the significance of rock ages in Cosmography.

The Periodic Table of the Species of Atoms

The third of our four tables is probably the most compact and meaningful compilation of knowledge that man has yet devised. *The periodic table of the chemical elements does for matter what the geological age table does for cosmic time.* Its history is the story of man's great conquests in the microcosmos. Following the pioneer work of Newlands,

Mayer, and especially Mendeléev, an inspired band of works in chemistry and physics has brought to essential completeness this basic categorizing of atoms.

The tabulation presents the now known species of atoms, arranged in vertical groups and horizontal series, and, when given in full display, supplies much information about atomic structure. The table encompasses all the kinds of matter, from the hydrogen of atomic number 1 through helium, carbon, iron, silver, gold, uranium (atomic number 92) up to the several unstable elements heavier than uranium which are creations of our atomic power houses. The last three are named for Einstein, Fermi, and Mendeléev.

Not only have the scientists of the past century constructed this complete two-dimensional coherent alphabet of matter but through the production and identification of scores of isotopes, they have produced for it a third dimension. *Thanks chiefly to the transmitting powers of the modern "atom-smasher", all the kinds of atoms can be made to appear in isotopic form,* that is, with variously weighted nuclei. For example, the naturally radioactive uranium atom may weigh either 238 or 235 units. Mercury has ten isotopes, seven of them stable. Tin has ten stable and seven radioactive isotopes. Many isotopes occur naturally; still more are only man made. Although the atomic weights differ for the various isotopes of an element, its outer structure of electrons, and therefore its chemical and spectroscopic properties, are essentially identical from one isotope to another.

For most of the elements the artificial isotopes, made in cyclotrons, are short-lived, vanishing through radioactive decay in small fractions of a second. *The dangerous hydrogen bomb by product, strontium 90, is, alas, not an evanescent isotope; for scores of years after its explosive creation it remains a poisonous menace.*

The radioactive isotopes of many common elements underlie the trace techniques that are now so potent in medical diagnosis and therapy, and in biological research. They are also increasingly important in geology. To use an analogy, we may say that the trace elements radium, lead, rubidium, etc., provide a diagnosis of the aging of rocks, and therefore, by way of fossil plants, provide a chart of the past vitality of the sun.

Without the principles and practical knowledge underlying the groups and series of the periodic table, the modern industrial age would not have been possible. And on the "impractical" side, no tabulation could better illustrate the value of the higher alphabets for the orientation of mankind in the material universe.

For various reasons the student of cosmic chemistry should be familiar with the bright stars and their spectra. The stars have influenced the philosophical thought of man from the earliest civilizations. They are at the beginning of man's lesson on his place in the universe. Also, they are high temperatured laboratories in which to test not only the properties of atoms but also the skill of the spectroscopic scientist.

More than sixty of the hundred kinds of atomic elements known on the earth's surface register also in the solar spectrum. The spectrum of stars is equally revealing. Doubtless the other elements exist in the sun and stars but are not easily detected. Many of the man-made isotopes, however, are probably terrestrial only, or, if in the sun, are not near the solar surface.

We have no evidence as yet of strange chemistries in the stellar laboratories scattered throughout space. The calcium and hydrogen atoms in the most remote of the receding galaxies appear to react as they do at the sun's surface and in the laboratories of terrestrial investigators. Even man-made technetium, number 43 of the periodic table, is now identified in the atmospheric spectra of some peculiar distant stars. Since technetium is radioactive with a relatively short life, it must be currently manufactured by some as yet undisclosed process near the stellar surface, perhaps in "star spots."

Throughout the accessible universe there appears to be a common chemical composition (though relative abundance differs from star to star); and everywhere similarity in atomic behavior prevails.

The World-Wide Argon Traffic

The helium, neon, argon, krypton, and other inert gases that line up in the last column of the periodic table are minutely present in our atmosphere. They remain entirely free of entangling alliances, unlike the atoms of oxygen and nitrogen which form combinations with many elements and particularly with the carbon on which life is built. Except for argon, these so-called noble gases appear only as traces, altogether about one-thousandth of one per cent of the earth's air.

In our atmosphere the atoms of argon, on the other hand, are about half of one per cent of the whole population of atoms. They are thoroughly mixed with the oxygen and nitrogen, and become a medium of exchange between all air breathers of the past, present, and future. They neither perish nor yield their individuality to molecular combinations. *They do not escape into interplanetary space as do the lighter atoms of hydrogen and helium.* Their origin is as one product of the natural radioactivity on one of the isotopes of potassium.

With each breath that we or any other man-sized animal breathes, forty-thousand million billion argon atoms are inhaled, and then, without loss, since they do not combine with anything, they are exhaled for rapid and thorough diffusion by the winds throughout the earth's atmosphere. Some of the argon atoms breathed in his first day by Adam (or any early man) *are in the next breath of all of us.* Some of the argon of our today's breathing will be in the first gasp of all infants a century hence. This argon traffic is obviously rich in suggestions; it implies a droll one-worldness and, like sunshine, recognizes no national boundaries. It links us with the breathing animals of the remote past and distant future in a sort of communal way.

The Ether Spectrum—An Alphabet for Energy

A table that simplifies the consideration of energy will complete the collection of major cosmographic aids. Such a tabulation is derivable from the so-called ether spectrum, *or electromagnetic spectrum of radiation.* It is not as comprehensive and satisfactory as the tables available for space, time and matter. There are energies, gravitational and mechanical, that are not directly included in the radiation sequence. But for exploring and understanding the total universe the most revealing energies are recorded in the electromagnetic spectrum. It was radiant energy that made possible the origin of terrestrial life and its continuation. Our existence, our warmth, our food, and most of our knowledge now depend in the solar energy transmitted through a short section of the other spectrum. (Atavistic sun worship should be natural for us.)

We should note, with high respect for man's intellect and industry, that he himself with artificial sense organs has extended the recognizable visual sequence far beyond that known throughout all human history until a century ago. His knowledge and use of radiant energy is no longer confined to the small violet-to-red segment. It ranges beyond the violet through untraviolet and X radiation to gamma rays. It goes beyond the red and infra red to radio and to the macrowaves of the light and power services of home and industry. His supplementary "sense organs" that permit this extension include photographic emulsions, thermocouples, photon tubes, transistors, oscilloscopes, Geiger counters, cloud chambers, and a maze of other electronic gadgetry. Pretty good for a recently arrived primate!

The full discussion of energy as a fundamental entity would include many recent scientific developments of relevance to Cosmography. It would detail the steps taken by physicists, astronomers, and engineers in extending spectrum analysis down into the short wave high-energy radiations. It would report how man's visual organs, the eyes, have been gradually supplemented by the ingenious accessories noted above. Nature's provision has been far transcended.

Scores of hitherto untouchable octaves of the electro-magentic spectrum, to left and right, have been explored. X-rays were discovered sixty years ago and quickly put to use to advance human health and human knowledge. This invisible ultraviolet ray has become a tool of industry and medicine and an aid to research into the nature of molecules and of biological cells. Equally great human service and in-dustrial developments have resulted from the extension of that original one octave of visual light into the realm of the longer waves. *The radioradar developments in the long wave lengths and the explosive energies of the gamma rays in the ultra-short wave lengths have created a new culture—the atomic civilization.* In a few short decades the exploration of the entities Energy and Matter has changed the human way of life and has deeply affected man's social philosophy. It is one thesis of this essay that these scientific discoveries and the techniques built upon them, may have destined the older philosophies and creeds to substantial readjustments; they point to the possibility of radical modificatons of some of the basic tenets. This idea is indirectly elaborated in later chapters.

The radiation spectrum is involved in many other out-standing developments such as (1) the penetration of the ozone layer in the earth's atmosphere by the war-inspired rockets; (2) *the modern alchemy of transforming one atom into another through bombardment with high energy proton, neutrons,* and *other corpuscles;* and (3) the fission of heavy atoms and the fusion of lighter ones in the interest of providing atomic energy for beneficent peace and male-ficent war.

Some of these items we must later sort out from the abundance provided by the electromagnetic spectrum and examine them in the interest of present interpretations in Cosmography and for future predictions. They should help in the placement problem.

Lesser Tables for Cosmography

The four major tabulations can advantageously be supplemented by a few other summarizing aids. Some of them are embodied in the subdivisions of the major tables—for example, the types of galaxies and the kinds of fundamental particles. *Five relatively small, useful tabulations are the following:*

(1) The planets of the solar system, their years, days distance, sizes—all of which are significant in the consideration of the origin of the earth.

(2) The major phyla of animals and plants; all of them are the terrestrial descendants of sunshine and the primeval "thin soup" of the shallow seas.

(3) Classes of mammalia, from whales to bats to cows and the anthropoids.

(4) The sequence of stellar spectra, a color and temperature progression from bluish hot Rigel in Orion to yellowish Canapus and the sun, and down the temperature scale to reddish Betelgeuse and Antares.

(5) Animal societies, a series from the salmon with her eggs, to the monogamous robin, to the buffalo herd, to human society, and on to the social integration achieved by honeybees and fungus-growing ants, which is the ultimate, perhaps, in social organization.

Summary of Orientations in Space, Time, Matter, and Energy

In concluding our review of the placement problem, let us see just where we stand with respect to the basic entities. We are dealing of course with the material universe. I hardly see how we can locate ourselves in what might be called the "stream of thought," or find our place in some mystical spiritual category. *We shall therefore summarize only in terms of our spot in time, space, energy, and matter.*

(1) Time: Obviously in time we are precisely between the past and the future. Concerning the future we can extrapolate a little, but cautiously. As far as planets, stars, and galaxies are concerned, we see clearly no end to the material universe; we can only guess on the authority of incomplete theories. Concerning the past, the indications are clearer that somewhere between five and fifteen billion years ago there was an epoch of extraordinary significance in the history of our physical world. We believe there was a specific creative moment, or epoch in the past, but no comparably specific moment in the future. We accept tentatively a finiteness in the past operation of an evolving universe, an infinity ahead.

Unless we deny to and assume that there was no "creation in time," no real beginning of the dust—and star-populated Metagalaxy, no start of the expanding universe, we must conclude that we are relatively young in time. Our days are not near the end of the world, nor even midway. The hydrogen fuel that heats the stars is very abundant. We—the galaxies, stars, organisms—are just getting under way. Our 10^{10} past years are brief, negligible of course compared with a future of eternity.

There is, to be sure, an alternative hypothesis. It holds that the explosion of the primeval superatom which contained everything is illusory, and that the past is "just as infinite" as the future. On this rather tentative hypothesis, which tastes a little of theology and ancient dogma, there must be a continuous creation (emergence) of matter out of nothing to make up for that which, because of the expansion of the material universe, is lost "over the rim of the world." The primeval atom theory is the suggestion of Canon Lemaitre; it is certainly consistent with many observations. *The "continuous creation" hypothesis is associated chiefly with the names of Jordon, Bondi, Gold* and *Hoyle;* it has yet to get the observational backing to match its esthetic appeal. For the present we can safely accept much past duration, and as much or more in the future.

(2) Space: We are more easily located in the size cate-

gory. It happens that man is just about as much larger than a hydrogen atom as the sun is larger than man. Geometrically, as we put it, we are in the middle register in the series of material bodies—that is *Star—Man*, Man—Atom; this is roughly true whether we are measuring in grams of mass or in centimeters of diameters. Man's location in space among the stars and galaxies is discussed in Chapter 7.

(3) Energy: To place ourselves somewhere in the energy table has practically no meaning. We would compute the amount of energy represented by the masses of our bodies and compare it with the energies represented by the masses of stars and atoms. But that comparison has largely no effect in finding our place in the organization of material systems. We could locate ourselves in a vague way through indicating the energy that we command, which seems to be tremendous compared with the resources of our forefathers. Now we have fuel-fed dynamos; we have hydroelectric plants, and recently we conquered at least a part of atomic energy. But if we add all these terrestrial sources together and claim that they represent our standing in the energy category, they would be nothing compared with a moment's radiation from an average star. It has been estimated that one substantial earthquake, which is neither man-made nor man-controlled is, energetically speaking, a fair-sized solar prominence making our "city-busters" dwindle to firecrackers dimensions, and is, energetically speaking, equal to a thousand atomic bombs. In short, in the total cosmic energy operation and potentiality, man and his works are of minor consequence.

(4) Matter: By taking a long term view we can claim a much better world position in the category of matter. Negligible and incidental though we may be in space, time, and energy, we do have the distinction of sharing a wide variety of chemical atoms with the greats of the universe—with inanimate planets, stars, galaxies, and cosmic dust. Man is in a sense of star stuff. Important in his composition are a score of the elements found in the earth's crust. *Some of the chem-*

ical elements are abundant in his body; others appear only as traces. The most prominent atoms in the makeup of animal bodies (mammalia) are the following, with an estimate of approximate percentage:

Oxygen	65%
Carbon	18
Hydrogen	10
Calcium	2
Phosphorus	1
Others	1

In the atmospheres of the sun and sunlike stars a current theory suggests the following distribution of matter:

Hydrogen	81.76%
Helium	18.17
Oxygen	0.03
Magnesium	0.02
Nitrogen	0.01
Silicon	0.006
Sulphur	0.003
Carbon	0.003
Iron	0.001
Others	0.001

And by another interpretation of astrophysical evidence and theory the sun's composition is this:

Hydrogen	87.0%
Helium	12.9
Oxygen	0.025
Nitrogen	0.02
Carbon	0.01
Magnesium	0.003
Silicon	0.002
Iron	0.001
Sulphur	0.001
Others	0.038

In the earth's crust, including air and oceans:

Oxygen	49.2%
Silicon	25.7
Aluminum	7.5
Iron	4.7
Calcium	3.4
Sodium	2.6
Potassium	2.4
Magnesium	1.9
Hydrogen	0.9
All others	1.7

But of the earth as a whole, which includes the hypothetical iron-nickel core, we have the following estimate of composition:

Iron	67%
Oxygen	12
Silicon	7
Nickel	4
Others	10

All of the many human-body elements are of course in or on the crust of the earth; most if not all of them have also been identified in the hot stellar atmospheres. *No atomic species is found in animal bodies that is not well known in the inorganic environment. Obviously man is made of ordinary star-stuff and should be mighty proud of it.*

In one respect animals and plants excel the stars. In the complexity of their molecules and molecular aggregates, living organisms transcend the atomic combinations of the inanimate world. *The sun's hot atmosphere and also the solar interior are found to be relatively simple in chemical structure when compared with the organic chemistry of a caterpillar. For that reason we are able to understand stars better than the larvae of insects.* The former operate chiefly under the gravitational, gaseous and radiation laws and are subject to the consequential pressures, densities, and temperatures. The organisms are hopeless mixtures of gases, liquids, and solids—hopeless, that is, from the standpoint of our working out for them neat and complete mathematical and physicochemical formulas. The astrophysicist has a simple job compared with the demands on the biochemist.

Before we can propose ourselves and our destiny as significant concerns of the universe, we should turn our attention to the possible existence and general spread of protoplasm throughout stellar spaces and cosmic times. *We can no longer be content with the hypothesis that living organisms are of this earth only. But before we ponder on the life spread,* we should inquire into the prevalence of suitable sites for biological operations. The initial question is not whether such sites are presently inhabited. *First, we ask: Are there other habitable celestial bodies—bodies that would be hospitable if life were there? No field of inquiry is more fascinating than a search for humanity, or something like humanity, in the mystery-filled happy lands beyond the barriers of interstallar space.* But are there such happy lands?

Other Stars, Other Planets

It is generally admitted by practical people that we exist. *Extremely few cogitators on this subject pretend to a suspicion that we do not, that it is all a dream, an illusion, a complicated fancy.* Let us go along with the majority and accept your existence and mine, and that of the physical world around us. And to simplify matters as a preliminary to discussion, let us say that the nonphysical world, if any, also exists. Around those words "nonphysical" and "exists" many battles could be fought, but the weapons would be mostly words, not ideas.

Since we exist on an earth where more than a million other kinds of animals are enjoying (or suffering) the same experience in biochemical evolution, we naturally meditate on the nature of this operation called living. We see a great variety of life forms and extreme diversity in loving conditions and not also the wide adaptability of man. *Naturally we ask: Are the likes of us elsewhere? The questions is directed sometimes to the pastor or the philosopher, but usually to the astronomer, and on behalf of astronomy I shall venture a reply, but in this chapter we consider chiefly the antecedent questions: Are planets like ours elsewhere?*

Human bodies are constructs of commonly known chemical elements, and nothing else. We have tabulated in the preceding chapter the principal atoms of the bodies of animals. The element oxygen accounts for about sixty-five percent hydrogen, three percent nitrogen, two percent calcium, and another two percent includes silicon, phosphorus, sodium, sulphur, iron, and a dozen other elements— all common to the crust of the earth and to the flames of the sun. The percentages vary somewhat from rat to leech, from watery octopus to crusty coral. There is more than average calcium in the bony vertebrates, more silicon in the brachiopods, more water in the jellyfish; but all animals employ all the common atoms. The elements uncommon to the rocks, like gold, platinum, and radium, are also uncommon to man (italics mine).

Now that we have heard from Dr. Shapley, let us also hear what other great thinkers had to say on the topic of ideas. The following are some quotations from *The Dictionary of Quotations* by Bergen Evans.

(1) He clepeth God the first cause (John Gower: Confessio Amantis III. lxxxviii, 1393)
(2) For science, God is simply the stream of tendency by which all things seek to fulfil the law of their being. (Matthew Arnold: Literature and Dogma I. iv)
(3) God . . . a gaseous vertebrate. (Ernest Haeckel: The Riddle of the Universe XV)

(4) Surely the Lord is in this place; and I knew it. (Genesis 28:16)

(5) Canst thou by searching find out God? (Job 11:7)

(6) They that go down to the sea in ships, that do business in great waters; These see the works of the Lord, and his wonders in the deep. (Psalms 107:23-24)

(7) No man hath seen God at any time. (John 1:10)

(8) Hath God obliged himself not to exceed the bounds of our knowledge? (Montaigne: Essays II. xii)

(9) It were better to have no opinion of God at all, than such an opinion as is unworthy of him: for the one is unbelief, and the other is contumely. (Francis Bacon *Of Superstition*)

(10) If God did not exist, it would be necessary to invent him. (Voltaire: Epitre a M, Saurin, Nov. 10, 1770)

(11) If God made us in His image, we have certainly returned the compliment. (Voltaire: LeSottisier XXXII)

(12) The nations are as a drop of a bucket, and are counted as the small dust of the balance: behold, he taketh up the ideas as a very little thing. (Isaiah 40:15)

(13) What hath God wrought! (Numbers 23:23)

(14) "There is no God," the wicketh saidth.
    "And truly it's a blessing.
For what he might have done with us
    It's better only guessing."
(Arthur Hugh Clough: Dipsychus I. v.)

(15) That God should spend His eternity which might be so much better employed—in spinning countless Solar Systems, and skylarking, like a child, with tops and teetotums—is not this a serious scandal? I wonder what all our circumgyrating Monotheists really do think of it? (Logan Pearsall Smith: *Trivia*, "Vertigo")

(16) If we assume that man actually does resemble God, then we are forced into the impossible theory that God is a coward, an idiot and a bounder. (H. L. Mencken: *Prejudices:* Third Series)

(17) An act of God was defined as something which no rea-

sonable man could have expected. (A. P. Herbert: *Uncommon Law*)

(18) Ye shall be as gods, knowing good and evil. (Genesis 3:5)

(19) Oh senseless man, who cannost possibly make a worm and yet will make Gods by dozen! (Montaigne: Essays II. xii.)

(20) 'Twas only fear first in the world made gods. (Ben Jonson: Sejanus II. ii.)

(21) When the gods were more manlike
Men were more godlike. (Schiller: Die Gotter Griechenlands)

So with the quotation in mind, we can see that ideas and knowledge vary when it comes down to some of the greatest topics of man. However, in my opinion the theory of M. E. C. = G shows all of us just how much we are apart, as well as everything in existence, known and unknown to us, such as, insects, reptile, quadrupeds, sea life, plant life, cosmic and astrological life, such as the constant birth of stars, suns, planets, moon, *and possibly other universe known and unknown to us—most of all, the constant reproduction by birth and the regeneration of the cells of man.* So you can see, we are a part of a gigantic massive energic cell, from which all creatures, man, and life spring and form, sustaining generating, and degenerating and finally deteriorating. *But with the atoms going right back to the main cause from which they came only to hook up again and produce something else, or that former kind of same mass, matter, or substance all over again. Therefore, this cell M. E. C. = G never uses itself up and will never end. Also, the M. E. C. = G works on the same or similar order as our sun.* The sun, which is just a speck in our universe and spinning top, though a giant of mass and matter, science tells us, works on this order.

The sun is a star around which all the planets of our solar system revolve. *It is a luminous mass of intense hot gases more than 300,000 times heavy as the earth and over 1,000,000 times larger. It is, in fact, our nearest star. (The nearest still means 93*

100

million miles away.) The sun is our only source of light and heat; without it, life as we know it would be impossible, and strangely enough much of the same elements are contained in the sun as in the earth and other planets, though in different proportions. *More than 99% of the sun is made up of hydrogen and helium,* but both of these elements are extremely rare on the earth as gases. The surface of the sun is exceedingly hot, *the actual temperature is around 6,000° C* and is hotter in the center where *the temperature is 20,000,000° C, though all we get from its heat is 0.000000000005 percent.* In the central powerhouse of the sun hydrogen atoms are continually combining to produce atoms of a heavier gas, helium. Each time an atom of helium is formed, energy in the form of light and heat is released, this is what makes the sunshine. In order to produce the amount of heat that the sun does, *some 600,000,000 tons of hydrogen must be converted into helium each second.* The sun has been doing this for at least 5,000,000,000 years, but its bulk is so great that no more than 5 percent of its hydrogen has been used up. So there is no danger of the sun running out of fuel for many, many million of years to come.

So when the many of millions of years are up, M. E. C. = G will suck up the atoms from our sun as it did before, some 5 million years ago, and produce another, which it is doing, so I believe in other universes and galaxies, unknown to us and yet to be explored. *So as the sun with its order of operation, so too is the order or similar order of M. E. C. = G.* But, as we can see, M. E. C. = G with its countless atoms and their makeup in which everything is apart, will never use itself up, and *as we renew some 3 billion cells each minute, then M. E. C. = G, with its own personal energy and intelligence, unknown to us, will continue to due the atoms cells of all things known and unknown to us.* Producing and reproducing, creating, activating, generating, degenerating, then deteriorating, *but converting them all over again into a thing or something and therefore continuing on and on. Could not M. E. C. = G be a kind of fifth dimension, while time could be the fourth?*

But, most of all, let us bear in mind that the massive energic cell is not just the cause of action and reaction or every chain reaction and every beginning an ending as found in the law of physics, metaphysics, biology, mathematics, chemistry, or every field of science. *But at the same token, other causes and action motion and emotion such as feelings as we know them and love, hate, good and evil, compassion, disgust, and the like.* Though these may seem like human attributes, they are at the same time actions of God and energy, M. E. C. = G, because all things known and unknown to us are contained in the M. E. C. = G. But, at the same time, this does not in any way sell Him or M. E. C. short. *If all life consists in part of all these things mentioned and not mentioned, then this is just another way of making M. E. C. = G more real. Life and death, as we know it, does not apply to Him per se* but at the same time is *manifested and controlled by Him.* Also, sex and form of any kind do not apply to Him. His indifference plus His supreme power over everything is what makes Him M. E. C., a cell of massive energy—God. He is God and always was and always will be God. We may say that God has no beginning, but this always is the proof of the smallness of man's mind. *For I say that He wasn't always but, like everything that He produced, came into being, and He or It knows that beginning, and He alone, no one else does.* By the same token, He was into being before all other things, so therefore, being before all others and creating by His massive energic power cell, all, each and every, we therefore, quite naturally apply no beginning to God or M. E. C. = G, or one in the same, or in part.

So, all in all, what we do have now in the new science of metaphysicotheologocosmologingoly, a three formula theorems:

1. Time of M = T = CG ÷ sec.
2. Time of M. E. C. = G
3. T = M. E. C. = G

1. Time of M = T = CG ÷ sec. has already been explained showing that M. E. C. = G, as a whole, is not manifest completely, but in part for the simple reason that (a) He, the massive

energic cell, is too big and, at the same time a fraction of its energy is in motivation and activation of the big 200 decillion mile spinning top, of 558,000 miles per second, even though this time top or capsule doesn't contain M. E. C. = G on a whole but only in part; (b) the massive energic cell is too big for the top, though activation of the top and not the top the M. E. C. = G and therefore time top or Time Capsule. Time is our time, but not M. E. C. = G's time.

2. Time of M. E. C. = G. Time, in this wise and as we know it, does not apply to M. E. C. = G for various reasons. (2) The M. E. C. doesn't need time for its existence, as other things do or have, *but time as its whole. Note as its whole,* not as we know it in form or some form such as lunar or solar or 60 seconds = 1 minute; 60 minutes = 1 hour, and so into days, weeks, months, and years upon years, or numbers in form or formula as we know and use them, or Faulkenstein's M = T = CG ÷ sec. *For this is another form of time, as we will I'm sure come to use and know, by so doing breaking the time barrier as applied to man and M = T = CG ÷ sec., but not when it comes to M. E. C. = G.* (b) *Time as its whole, as a thing that measures all things, yet all things cannot measure it, is in one or the same plus energy, the M. E. C.* (c) For time as a whole and the M. E. C. came into being *simultaneously.* Note, scientifically, this matter is T = M. E. C. = G. This is my third theory. T = M. E. C. = G *is a simultaneous equation, meaning in mathematics two or more equations satisfied by the same set of values of the unknown quantities.* So philosophically, this can be applied to T = M. E. C. = G, *meaning time is a massive energic cell equalling God. Both came into being at the same time,* knowing the secret of one another and both working in harmony with one another. *When applied to T = M. E. C. = G, they are both or in part one or the other, and for someone to try and find the beginning of time without God or God without time is humanly foolish and intellectually impossible.* However, if we choose to use them both together intellectually and scientifically as a simultaneous equation, *in the formula theorem T = M. E. C. = G, we no doubt could have the answer to both—Time and God.* And, if not,

then no one but a fool would reject this unless he had a theory or theories to equal or surpass $M = T = CG \div$ sec., M. E. C. $= G$, and $T = M. E. C. = G$. In our modern age or in the time of man, Faulkenstein's theories are due consideration. Until Faulkenstein's theories are used in one way or another, they will continue to show us that man and modern man is no doubt the most primitive form of higher life in the whole and entire universe.

However, in all forms of science, the scientist who conceives of an idea or a theory usually has a model of some sort to show—not always but most of the time. So my model to show you the truth of my theories is my mathematical word formula, and your imagination. So to help show or in some way prove God's existence, or $T = M. E. C. = G$, go in this way. *All things made require a maker, all things created require a creator, or all things having a being also have an ending, all things having an action have a reaction.* Now how are we going to apply this trend of thought to God and time? Time and God, to mankind, are so big and unmeasurable that we *have declared that time has no beginning or end but continues on and on.*

3. And since God is beyond our intelligence we say that He always was and always will be. To top it off, man's mind is so small that when it comes to a concept such as God or time that he has long made God into images that he could understand in one way, then another. To prove this, just check your religions of the world and you will find, as Michael deMontaigne did in the sixteenth century in his investigation, that took him half his life. He discovered that man has *invented, worshipped and created 3,600 gods in all and every image known to us and last of all Jesus Christ became after Ceasar the 3,601 god.* And what do these 3,601 gods show us during most of man's history? The Bible said, "God created man in his own image." And, now, over the course of man's history, *man has made God in his own image out of his mind,* meaning that man, out of his own imagination, had possibly created God instead of the Bible statement that God created man. But I said, possibly. God has already been discussed in both theories, $M. = T = CG \div$ sec. and M. E. C. $= G$; therefore, I need not go on.

4. Time. We have already discussed time, but I will elaborate just a little. Let's look at time briefly. Time, as I have said, is a thing that measures all things, yet all things cannot measure it. Time is a mystery to us as a thing in existence before us and by the same token unmeasurable as we know measurements. Time in its fullness has no form as we know forms, except for part, note a part, of time in the theory of $M = T = CG \div$ sec. Though I stated before that time, when applied to $M = T = CG \div$ sec., is round or circular in form, this spinning on and on and then forming a time continuum, as we know time, applies to us. Note the fourth dimension. But when this is applied to us; however, time in its fullness is like God; incomprehensible and beyond our greatest expectations. We ask them, where was the beginning of time? and God? And then trying to answer the beginning of one without the other is the same as if one would try and answer the questions, as to which came first, the chicken or the egg. If a person answered, "the egg," then the question would be, "Who laid the egg?" then we would be back to the chicken. Also, when it came to the question Which came first, the boy or the man the results would be the same. *The same applies when* it comes to time or God. $T = M. E. C. = G$ shows us that *one is really no good without the other. They are both one or in part the same, with God being the first cause. Time and God are the same*, when time is applied to all things known and unknown to us; light, and sound. The theory that the whole universe was in musical harmony, when applied to sound, was stated by Johannes Kepler (1571-1630). Though other scientists of his day and our day have not, you may say, researched into this field to reduce this to truth or false, I would say that where there is any form of movement or vibration, this would have to produce some form of sound, though perhaps not heard by us. Yes, Mr. Kepler, you are right, the whole universe is singing, and in so doing, these stars, planets, suns, satellites, in their fashion, are praising the first cause: $M. E. C. = G$ or $T = M. E. C. = G$, Anything that vibrates and consist of some form of movement in time, giving off some form of sound, that is to say that any planet, star, comet, meteorite, etc., with their movement and

105

energy at the same time not giving off sound, would be the same as to say objects of color have no color.

So when we look at things in this fashion, we can see that there is sound or some form of musical harmony all throughout the universe and universes known and unknown to us. Not to stray from the main point, which was and is God and time, T = M. E. C. = G or M. E. C. = G. I just thought I'd mention sound because it is such a part of our daily life and the three theories at hand. So, once again, how can we prove that God and time are the same and equal? Note M. E. C. = G and T = M. E. C. = G; this is all very simple and can be summed up in this wise: (1) *to say that God has no beginning, as I stated before, is foolish and primitive;* (2) *to try and place God without time and time without God is also primitive and backward;* (3) to say that God always was is old-fashioned, backward, and primitive; and (4) time without God and God without time is impossible. *Because one is no good without the other.*

Now read and think of what I am about to say very carefully. *To take all time and any form of time from God, such as no beginning and no ending, would make God nonexistent.* Everything that exists came into being in some form of time, *No matter what it is, and this means God, too.* Because if we took all time from a thing, anything, *it would not exist.* If we add an unconditional time without limit to a thing, anything, then this would in a sense *make it always, preexistent.* Since it needs to come into being, to be, *then there is no preexistence of anything.* So all in all, time once again is the main factor, and since M. E. C. = G has already been explained, then T = M. E. C. = G or M. E. C. = T and G. To talk of God or think of God without time is senseless because, once again, the thought of God being always without time shows us that He wouldn't exist at all. Because time is unmeasurable, to us it is the same as God, since *they are both beyond our expectation.* Since they are both beyond us and before us, in the existence of things, we say, with our primitive mind and thought, *they have no beginning nor end. Time knows God's beginning, and God knows time's beginning because they are one in the same.* God and time

106

can be likened to the wheel of perpetual motion. The wheel will spin on and on, but first of all it needs a push. So God will be forever as long as there is such a thing as time itself. *God had a beginning; the only thing is we don't know that beginning.* So we're right; if time does not apply to God as a "beginning" in some form, He always was (and always will be) nonexistent. But God is M. E. C. $=$ G. Time is also a part of M $=$ T $=$ CG $\div$ sec. Then T $=$ M. E. C. $=$ G. *They came into being simultaneously, one knowing the secret of the other.* By the same token, one being no good without the other, one relative to the other. One is the other; T $=$ M. E. C. $=$ G or M. E. C. $=$ G $=$T.

Fig. 1. FAULKENSTEIN'S MODEL OF THE MOLECULER-STRUCTURE OF THE *ABSTRACT*-ENERGIC *ATOM*.

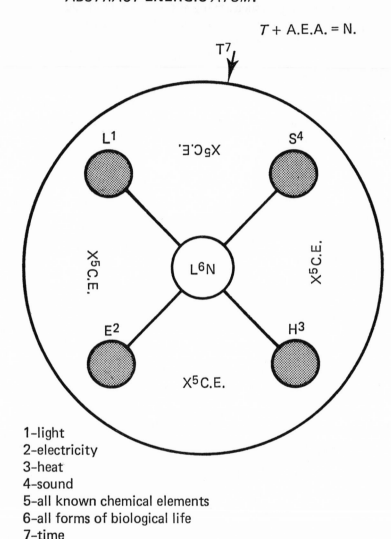

T + A.E.A. = N.

1–light
2–electricity
3–heat
4–sound
5–all known chemical elements
6–all forms of biological life
7–time

A–model of the first (laws) of nature

13

The First Law of Nature
(T + A. E. A. = N)

The first law of nature for centuries now has been thought, taught, and believed to be self-preservation. However, as a scientist, philosopher, and metaphysician, I am forced to shatter, overturn, and upset this false conception and thus give to the world and mankind a pinch of truth through physics, philosophy, metaphysics, and science—*Better still, my own science metaphysico-theologocosmologingology.*

So, to begin, for us to believe in that old and worn-out lie that the first law of nature is self-preservation is to remain backward, small-minded, old-fashioned, and primitive. The reason for this stupidity and ignorance can be found in my metaphysical formula theorem T + A. E. A. = N, *meaning time plus an abstract energic atom equals nature.* We can get a better understanding of this by looking at or studying my model of the first laws of nature, in which is shown the molecular structure of the abstract energic atom. With the previous model we can see that there is truly no first (law) of nature but truth laws. The first Laws of Nature number from one to seven. Faulkenstein's model shows us in chronological order that these laws are from one to seven concerned with time. They are: 1. light; 2. electricity, 3. heat, 4. sound, 5. all known chemical elements, 6. all forms of biological life, and 7. time, the forerunner of them all. That is what I mean by time, one to seven, that 1 time brought them, along with their own laws, into being and time measures all things, yet all of them cannot measure time and do not measure time. If they do, then it is only in part, a part of time only and not time per se.

Second, the molecular structure of the A. E. A. (abstract energic atom) = N (nature) shows it is in physics twofold. *The number "1" to "4" are energy and "5" and "6" are matter and "7" time,* is neither. Therefore, *it would be abstract, giving us an abstract energic atom.* Also, we could use the term *energic* atom due to the fact that in science, physics, metaphysics and philosophy, time would be, I believe, closer to the laws of energy than to matter. So, once again, *time is neither energy nor matter but has its own law per se.* It is abstract. Thus, the (n) nature of this atom of energy, matter, and time is unlike our regular atom of an electron, proton, and neutron.

Third, we see from this that there is no first law of nature, but laws. To say or state a first law is to be philosophical or metaphysical. But in plain science dealing with nature, per se, and not just a part of it, then physics comes into play. For the word and meaning of physics is from the Greek word *physicos*, meaning nature. Philosophy, deals with the natural and material world, but the Science of Physics deals with the science of phenomena of lifeless matter involving no chemical change. This is nature and laws of nature and not, as we think, or have been lead to think and believe, that this only applies to some biological form of life in constant struggle to survive. In so doing to act, think, and move for this or that individual being. That form of law does not include all of nature, only a speck of it. For a person to place his thoughts, beliefs, and mind into this speck, like Darwin did, is to miss the real and true physics or nature as well as its laws. So now we can see that there is no first law of nature but laws, and that the first law of nature is an abstract energic atom, with the makeup, building blocks, or molecular structure of light; electricity; heat; sound; all known chemical elements; nucleus, all form of biological life and time, engulfing them all.

110

The molecular structure of the abstract energic atom would be in much brighter terms, a gigantic circle consisting of molecules with light; electricity; heat; sound; all form of biological Life; between the 4 molecules filling the space would be all known chemical elements, and unknown. The gigantic circle that has engulfed them and sealed them would be time.

Therefore, we know now that the first law of nature is an abstract energic atom consisting of matter, energy, and time. This would be $T + A. E. A. = N$, meaning time plus an abstract energic atom equals nature because it is nature!

14

Space and Interplace

Space? Space and our traveling through it and just looking at it, is only our own individual illusion. Such as, let's use the Model of U —— D, or I —— O. U-for up; D-for down; I-for in; and O-for out, plus the line between will be used for what we call space. Now let's go back first to our basic three dimensions. 1. to go up or down; 2. to go from side to side; 3. to go forward and backward. Nos. 1, 2, and 3 are on the one plane, a line from one point to another. So nothing has changed the pattern of the line from U to D or I to O, only the way in which you would travel. *Any three of these ways would still be on one plane, a line only*. Such as U and D are equal to I and O, such as C to C equal to side to side, or U to D equal up or down and F to B equal forward and backward, *still all of them are on one plane, a line*. And what does all of this boil down to? We can see the one plane with two points or more. And from point U to D is not outer space but out of place. *Out of one place to another*. What would we call the line from point U to D not space but interplace. If we are in between U and D, and if we should go outside of U to D, still this is not outer space, but one of one place into another, from point U to D. So once again we have no outer space and no space at all but only outer place or interplace. Interplace is nothing more, as I have said before, the line between two points or more. So we should deal more with inter-and outer place and dismiss what we all call space altogether.

15

The Numbers Two and Three

The question may be asked as to why I would use the term and numbers *two and three, to explain the velocity of Time*. Such as the statement in the theory, Time is two to three times faster than light. The reason is that we are dealing with, first, of all, *the two basic things out of three*, that we feel we know more about, and they are sound and light. About *the third, time, we know less*. Also, we have yet to learn more about the three of them as a whole. The number 2 we know means many things to us, such as the philosophical two of things: good and bad; right and wrong; heaven and hell; woman and man; night and day; up or down; action and reaction, etc. *So 2 is nothing but the basic difference or similarity of a thing* (plus² = the square root, in mathematics).

The number three goes in this wise. *Three was the perfect number of the philosopher Pythagoras.* It is expressive of "beginning, middle, and end," wherefore he makes it a symbol of deity. *A trinity is by no means confined to the Christian creed.* The Hindu trinity consists of Braham, the Creator, Vishnu, the Preserver, and Siva, the Destroyer. The world was supposed, by the ancient Greeks, to be under the rule of three gods: Zeus (heaven), Poseidon (sea), and Hades (underworld). The Fates are three, the Furies three, the Graces three, the Harpies three, the Sibylline books three times three (of which only three survived); the fountain from which Hylas drew water was presided over by three

113

nymphs; the Muses were three times three; the pythoness sat on a three-legged stool, or tripod; and in Scandinavian mythology we hear of the Mysterious Three: Har the Mighty, the Like-Mighty, and the Third Person, who sat on three thrones above the rainbow.

Man is threefold (body, soul, and spirit); the world is three-fold (earth, sea, and air); the enemies of man are three fold (the world, the flesh, and the devil); the Christian graces are threefold (faith, hope, and charity); the kingdoms of nature are threefold (mineral, vegetable, and animal); the cardinal colors are three in number (red, yellow, and blue), and so on. So this is why the numbers two and three were selected.

So I would like to say in closing that I have already agreed with the man who once said that *the mind is the soul talking with itself*. And the other man who said that man learns more and more about less and less until by and by he has learned everything about nothing.

So consider my three theories, one will find them in the fields of physics, metaphysic, theology, cosmology, and mathematics, in short, metaphysicotheologocosmologingology. And to those people in these fields of study, I hope they will be appreciated, but for the more religious person, I have enclosed for you some passages from the Holy Scripture, and for the agnostic, I give you my respect. And, as for the atheist, I hope that in my theory you can discover God, and most of all rediscover yourself. If you wish not be an atheist, then know one thing for sure, *that we and all things in this big universe of our are but a speck riding on the ass of time*. Note $M = T = CG \div$ sec. And for the fool, I say to you that a wise man will speak because he has something to say, but a fool will speak because he just has got to say something.

My thought are not your thoughts; or Isa. 45:5-7; 45:16-25; 55:8; 46:4-8-9-10; Prov. 1:1-33; Job 11:7.
A few scriptures from the Bible about knowing God:
Job 8:9, Ps. 73:11; 59:9; 103:14; Jer. 31:34 and Hos. 2:20
A few scriptures on seeking God:

Deut. 12:5; 2 Chron. 15:2; Ps. 53:1-2; Isa. 8:19; 34:16;
Rom. 3:11; 1 Cor. 1:22; Col. 3:11; Heb. 11:6
Understand:
Prov. 20:24; Jer. 9:24, Matt. 24:15; Prov. 8:1

However, with $M = T = CG \div$ sec., M. E. C. $= G$ and $T = $ M. E. C. $= G$, we shouldn't just say we have a new formula theorem of time, mass, space, man, and the universe but also a modern evolutionary writing or thought, a believable or unbelievable new idea, or simply a great idea if nothing else. So with this in mind, if the theory of $M = T = CG \div$ sec., M. E. C. $= G$, T. $= $ M. E. C. $= G$, and T. $+$ A. E. A. $= N$ don't belong in the field of physics, then put them in the field of metaphysics, and if not there, then in philosophy or natural philosophy, and if not there in science and then in science fiction, then if not there, then simple fiction. And if all these fields reject them, then place them on a shelf as one of the many great lies to have ever been written by man.

Bibliography

Barnett, Lincoln. *The Universe and Dr. Einstein*. New York: Bantam Books, 1957.

Bennet, William Rose. *The Reader Encyclopedia*, 2nd ed. New York: Thomas Y. Crowell Co., 1965.

Bergamini, David, et al. *The Universe*. New York: Time-Life Books, 1966.

Clark, Ronald. *Einstein—The Life and Times*. New York: World Pub. Co., 1971.

Coleman, James A. *Relativity for the Layman*. New York: Signet Books, 1958.

The Columbia Viking Desk Encyclopedia. New York: Viking Press, 1960.

Cung, Hilaire. *Albert Einstein, the Man and His Theory*. New York: Fawcett Publications, 1962.

Dempsey, Michael, and Pick, Joan. *The Majesty of Heaven*. New York: Greystone Press.

Durant, Will. *The Story of Philosophy*. New York: Simon and Schuster, 1935.

Evans, Bergen, *Dictionary of Quotations*. New York: Delacorte Press, 1968.

Freeman, Ira M. *Physics Made Simple*. Made Simple Books. New York: Greystone Press, 1957.

The Great books. Chicago: University of Chicago Press.

Ibanez, Felix Marti. "Atomic Science and Modern Art." *M.D., the Medical Newsmagazine*, Vol. 12, no. 11, p. 9.

Karp. Walter. *Charles Darwin and the Origin of Species*. New York: American Heritage, 1968.

Margenan, Henry, and Bergamini, David. *The Scientist.* New York: Time-Life Books, 1964.
Moore, Ruth. *Evolution.* New York: Time-Life Books, 1962.
Nourse, Alan E. *The Body.* New York: Time-Life Books, 1964.
Shapley, Harlow. *Of Stars and Men.* Boston: Beacon Press, 1959.